Not Your Parents' Offering Plate

Not Your Parents' Offering Plate

A New Vision for Financial Stewardship

J. CLIF CHRISTOPHER

Abingdon Press
Nashville

NOT YOUR PARENTS' OFFERING PLATE
A NEW VISION FOR FINANCIAL STEWARDSHIP

This book is printed on acid-free paper.

Library of Congress Cataloging-in-Publication Data

Christopher, J. Clif.
    Not your parents' offering plate : a new vision for financial stewardship / J. Clif Christopher.
        p. cm.
    ISBN 978-0-687-64853-5 (binding: pbk., adhesive, perfect : alk. paper)
    1. Stewardship, Christian. I. Title.
    BV772.C47 2008
    254'8—dc22

                                                                    2008012673

09 10 11 12 13 14 15 16 17—10 9 8 7 6 5 4
MANUFACTURED IN THE UNITED STATES OF AMERICA

CONTENTS

120510

WHY I READ THIS BOOK AND WHY YOU SHOULD TOO

Many people are running around today claiming to be fund-raisers. Some are and some aren't. Clif Christopher is the real deal. I've known Clif from the time he began Horizons Stewardship Company. I've had the privilege of watching him grow into one of the finest human beings I know. If you want to learn how to raise money from a man of character, this is the book for you.

Raising money by using an outside consultant can be a tricky business. Unless you really know the person you have invited into your shop, you run a huge risk. If you don't get someone with great integrity, you can be in a lot of trouble.

I can still remember what it was like being a pastor in a growing church—we always needed more money. No matter how much we raised, it was never enough. So, I've used fund-raisers time and time again, and one thing stands out

about every one of them: the character of the person raising the money. It was always crucial—the person can make
or break the effort. That's just one of the reasons this is an
important book for anyone responsible for raising money in
a church—Clif is a man of integrity.

It's not as easy to raise money today as it was in the
past. Times have changed and many people who teach
stewardship haven't changed with the times. Clif Christopher has. I've watched Clif's company grow into one of the
most noble and consistently effective companies in the field
of Christian fund-raising. If you want to learn from someone who has effectively raised funds in all types of situa-
tions, this book is for you.

I don't write many forewords for books, but I'm honored to do this one because it's not often that I can write
such glowing words about a person or a company. Con-
tained within the pages of this book are insights that need
to be read and understood by every pastor. It contains the
up-to-date wisdom of someone who is not only a practi-
tioner of the faith but also of someone who is steeped in
the fund-raising skills and gifts used by leaders of the best
nonprofit organizations in the world.

TROUBLE BREWING

Every year people give away billions of dollars, with religion being the largest recipient of those donations. One

would think that that's great. But hold on. In 2006, Americans gave 295 billion dollars—an increase of 1 percent above the rate of inflation. The numbers were disappointing considering the stock market had double-digit gains during the same period.

But that's not the worst news. In 2006, for the first time in recorded history, gifts to religion fell below 33 percent of charitable giving. Just twenty years ago, gifts to religion amounted to nearly 60 percent of all charitable giving. Not so any longer. Every year, religion continues to get a smaller piece of the charitable pie because church leaders simply do not know how to compete for the charitable dollar. Not only that, some leaders don't think they should compete, as if the Lions Club was as important as the Great Commission.

The church is now just one of many organizations competing for a piece of the charitable-dollar pie. In order to be effective, we have to learn why people of today give and what the church can do to compete with other charitable organizations.

In the following pages, Clif will show you the way to effective fund-raising. The book is full of practical, down-to-earth suggestions and applications. And Clif doesn't pull any punches.

Pastors cannot afford to bury their heads in the sand and pretend they're in competition not only for the souls of humanity but also for that which makes the world go round—money. I don't think you can. If I were still a local church pastor, this book would be on my desk, not in the bookshelf. That's how good it is.

Bill Easum

Cofounder, Easum, Bandy and Associates

www.easumbandy.com

INTRODUCTION

When I completed my seminary education, I was sent to a church that wanted to relocate to a larger plot of ground. This sounded like a good idea to me since the current church occupied a small portion of one block and had about four parking spaces. A couple of weeks after the congregation and I had gotten acquainted, a meeting was called with the building committee. We talked through the relative merits of doing this move, and then one of the leaders turned to me and said, "Well, how are we going to get the money?" I just stared at him like a deer in the headlights. I did not have a clue. I told them that I was sure our denominational headquarters would have some good ideas, and we adjourned with my assignment to call them and bring forth a credible plan.

Much to my surprise, I did not find any readily available sources of help; I would be left to my own devices. I had completed three years of graduate education to be a minister in the church and no one had taught me one thing about money—how to raise it, invest it, or manage it. I turned to persons I knew in the nonprofit world and tried to adapt some of their knowledge to the church. At the time, I did not understand how or why, but the basic plan worked and our little church raised enough money to relocate and expand its ministry.

In their wisdom, my denominational bosses decided that I should then go to another place and then another place—all who needed to build and raise funds. At each place, I fumbled along making countless mistakes but somehow achieving the end result of facilities and the monies to pay for them.

Thus was born, in 1992, the Horizons Stewardship Company to work with congregations doing what I had been doing for nearly twenty years of pastoral ministry. By that time I had been to numerous schools and professional seminars to learn the craft of raising money in the church. I thought I really knew it all. Very quickly I realized that I did not know half of what I needed to know to be truly effective. My approach was still similar to what had been done in Christian financial stewardship for years and years. I was not doing anything very different from what was done in my parents' church and their parents' church before them. Two dramatic events happened in quick succession to show me that no longer was it my parents' offering plate.

When Horizons was about a year old, I attended a philanthropy meeting. Most of the major philanthropists of my home state were at this meeting. A young attorney was asked to be the keynote speaker because it had recently been revealed that he was giving 1.5 million dollars to a local youth center. His speech was dynamic and I was struck by his sincerity and conviction. It was filled with faith references and it was obvious to me that his spiritual convictions were a driving force in his desire to make his magnanimous gift.

As soon as I got out of the meeting, I returned to my office, I called the attorney's office and asked for an appointment. Graciously, he gave me a time to come in the next day. After a couple of pleasantries, I asked him to explain to me why he would make such a gift.

I can still see him leaning forward excitedly in his chair. He began to share with me the story of a young, inner-city boy from a broken home with seemingly no hope, who had gotten involved in the center and how it had completely turned his life around. Now that boy was on his way to college with wonderful plans to return to his neighborhood and make a difference. By the time the attorney finished, he was just beaming with excitement. He said, "I asked the director what could be done to create more stories like this and he quickly told me that he needed a new center but one would cost 1.5 million dollars. I thought to myself, 'Well I have 1.5 million dollars and that would be a great way to use it. If he can change lives, I can fund it.'"

Then I shifted gears with him a bit and asked him his church involvement. He told me that he was very active in his local church, attending about forty-eight Sundays a year.

I asked him if he gave to the church and his answer was revealing. "I give as good as most," he replied. Then I asked him if he would ever consider giving a gift like he gave to the center, to his church. He stared right at me and said, "Lord, no, they wouldn't know what to do with it."

Later in the conversation he told me that he was going to give a million dollars away the next year to another youth organization. Because of his earlier comment, I asked him point-blank if he thought this youth organization was doing more for young people than his church's denomination (that had about thirty churches in the community). He quickly answered, "Oh yeah, without a doubt!"

Here was a young, active church member who, though highly motivated to give, was not highly motivated to give to his church. What were we missing? What was this man saying to me that my churches needed to hear? I believe that the church is the one institution that has the potential to change the world, and this man is active in the church, but he does not want to give to it. How can I reach persons like him? This conversation began a frantic search by me to see where we had gone wrong in appealing to this type of donor. It would be fair to say that everything I hope to teach in this book has sprung from this one conversation.

I subsequently went out and intentionally had other conversations with active church people about why they were giving and what they truly thought of giving to their church, and found my young attorney to not be an exception. This attitude was much closer to the norm. It was not my parents' offering plate anymore.

About a year later, I was asked to help a small, faith-based college located near our office with a capital campaign. This was new territory for me. I had started my company to work with churches, because church work was my background. I had been to numerous schools and learned how nonprofits worked and how capital campaigns should be run, but I had never served as a fund-raiser for a school before. So I enlisted the help of a man, a national leader in collegiate philanthropy, to give me some guidance on the side. By working with this knowledgeable man and talking to countless potential donors, I learned how donors think and why they give (or don't give). It struck me how most of the potential donors for the college were active church members who were often choosing to give the college a large donation, while giving a much smaller one to their church. I spent countless hours talking to them about their reasons for making the choices they were making. The most enlightening comment came near the end of the campaign, when one lady who had made a six-figure contribution to the college said to me, "You know, I was at the college for four years, and I have been a member of my church for forty. No one at the church has ever treated me like they do at the college. I really matter here, and I want to help them all I can."

These persons who wound up giving millions to this small college love their Lord. What so many of them were saying to me paralleled the words of that young attorney. They believe that Jesus is hard at work changing lives in youth centers and on college campuses and in many cases getting much more done there than in the church. They are going to send their money where they see the most results. Yet, today what I see in most churches is a message that simply says, "Give us money because we need it—NOW!" And we wonder why we are not getting more. Well, my friends, this is not your parents' offering plate anymore.

In the following pages, I hope to detail what I have learned and to share with you what most of our churches have not yet realized but must if they have any hope of succeeding in the years ahead.

CHAPTER ONE

SURVIVAL OF THE FITTEST

In America today, there are over 1.8 million nonprofit organizations, and over one million of these are 501(c)(3)s. There are about 370,000 churches. Just ten years ago, in 1995, there were 600,000 501(c)(3)s and about 370,000 churches. What these numbers show is that in ten years the competition has nearly doubled.

The Number of 501(c)(3) Organizations 1996–2006

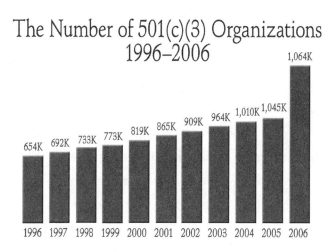

Source: Giving USA Foundation™ / *Giving USA 2007*

Each year finds the number of nonprofits in America growing by anywhere from 5 to 7 percent. Their numbers are increasing much faster than charitable giving. As more and more organizations vie for fewer and fewer dollars, someone has to lose. All cannot thrive equally. Sadly, in many instances the loser has been the church, because churches have been blind to the fact that they must compete. When I first got to college, there was one drive-in eating establishment in our town. They had burgers and foot-long hot dogs. We would drive up, wait for someone to come out to the car to take our order, and in ten or fifteen minutes we would get some food. It wasn't great food and it wasn't great service, but it was OK for our little town. Well, by the time I graduated, there was a McDonald's and a Burger King. A couple of pizza places opened up and we had choices. The little burger joint never changed the way it did business, even though the competition around them changed dramatically. Within a year, it closed, never to open again. Their burger used to be good enough. What happened? Why did the customers start going elsewhere?

The very same thing is happening in the charitable world. The church used to be the predominant charity in most communities. In many, it was the only place to make a contribution of any kind. The appeal was simply, "You should give." And people would heed the appeal and give. For too many churches the appeal is still "you should give."

And people respond by giving, just not to the church. They are hearing the preacher say that Jesus wants them to give, and they are choosing the youth center or the college or the hospital. Yet, our appeal is still the same. We must learn to answer the question our donors are asking us, "Why should I give to YOU?"

According to *Giving USA 2007*, giving to religion amounted to 32.8 percent of all charitable giving in 2006. This was by far the largest category for charitable contributions, beating education, which got 13.9 percent. On the surface this looks like very good news for those of us in the church business. We seem to be America's favorite charity. But there is a problem. Our piece of the pie is shrinking at an alarming rate.

In 1985, religion received 53 percent of all charitable contributions. Through the 1990s religion received around 40 to 45 percent.

By 2000 the percent had dropped below 40 percent and it continues to fall. Donors are showing us that though we are still number one, we are rapidly falling out of favor. They are continuing to give, just not to the churches.

As noted in *Giving USA*, "Since 2001, giving to religion has shown a rate of growth of 3.6 percent, while disposable personal income has increased more than 8 percent (adjusted for inflation)." People have the money and they continue to give. Religion is just no longer their charity of choice.

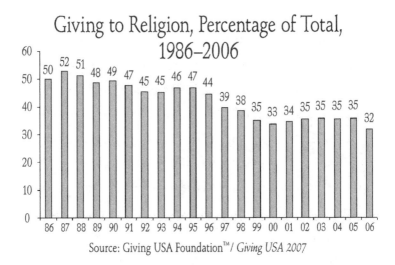

Giving to Religion, Percentage of Total, 1986–2006

Source: Giving USA Foundation™ / *Giving USA 2007*

I visited with a woman not too long ago whose family was very wealthy. She was a gifted businesswoman who was paid highly for her expertise. Her husband owned an oil company that had exploded with growth during the "high gas price" years. They had belonged to their church for over thirty years and had held every major lay office in the church. During my visit, the wife shared with me a recent conversation that she had had with her pastor.

"Last year my husband and I gave a million-dollar gift to the local hospital. It was announced in the newspaper and thus became common knowledge around the church. It became somewhat obvious to us after this that our pastor was looking at us a bit differently than he had before. One day I asked him to come over and the two of us talked about what was going on. He did not want to own up to his feelings at first, but finally he said as politely as he could, 'I just do not know why you have not made a gift to the church like the one you gave to the hospital.'

"I proceeded to tell him how the gift came about, as a way of showing him why they got the gift and he did not. I told him how the CEO of the hospital had personally come out to see my husband and me on several occasions to seek our advice about the new wing. He asked us to join the board that was designing the center. During nearly every one of our meetings, he shared the case as to why this new wing was necessary, how it would change lives and make our community a much better place to live. One day he came on his own, sat in our living room and asked us for one million dollars, to be the lead gift in the campaign. Once we agreed, we got the most wonderful letter from him, along with a framed rendering of the new wing. Around the mat board of the rendering were the signed thank-yous of each nurse who will work in the center. We hung it up in our study. The picture certainly surprised us, but the thank-you letter did not. We always got one whenever we have made a gift, of any size, to the hospital. It has just been a joyous experience for us both."

She looked at me and finally said, "I am not sure if he understood how different this experience has been from what we experience with the church. He just thanked me and left."

This woman and her husband are fine Christian people, whose giving has been shaped by their Christian convictions. They give, in many respects, as stewards who perceive that all they have has been given to them by God and they have a responsibility to their Creator to give back. At the same time, because they are stewards who believe that God holds them accountable for their giving, they want to be sure their gift is used wisely and truly makes a difference. The hospital helped convince them that the gift would be used well , to change lives, while the church simply said, "Why don't you give to us?"

To compete is not something most of our churches are prepared to do, and many even resent the implication that they should. Along with many others, I have watched as the mainline church has declined for over three decades. In the early years, part of the reason for the decline was the idea that competition was somehow unchristian. Fifty years ago, most of our country had blue laws that prohibited businesses from opening on Sunday. Many towns closed up on Wednesdays to leave this open as "church night." Then the laws changed and people started having options. Even youth ball games were being scheduled on Sunday mornings. I heard many a church complain but few towns have reinstated blue laws and Wednesday is just like every other day of the week now.

The churches that survived this onslaught did not just sit around and protest that people were not coming. They went out and proceeded to earn people's time and attention. Worship was outstanding and youth meetings became dynamic. They were willing to lay their case right up against the soccer teams and say to the parents, "Look what we have to offer. Wouldn't you rather have your kid here?" Not only did the parents want their kids to go there, the kids preferred it also. The churches took on the competition, believing that their product could be superior, and won.

Donors are saying to our churches today that you have to earn our gifts. No longer can you just preach a sermon on tithing and think the members will give 10 percent to the church. They will hear your message that tithing is what God wants them to do, and then they will go home and decide to give the church 2 percent, the youth center 2 percent, the homeless shelter 2 percent, and their college 4 percent. They will then look you right in the eye when you say that it all should go to the church, and they will ask you, "Do you not believe that Jesus is working in the youth center and the homeless shelter and with our college students?" If you are not prepared to compete with over one million nonprofits, you will lose.

Just a few years ago the Oldsmobile brand of General Motors began a series of ads stating, "It's not your father's Oldsmobile." The reason they were running the ads was that sales of Oldsmobiles had declined steadily for a number of years. The perception in the marketplace was that the Olds was for the senior set, not for anyone under 60.

They tried at the last minute to change the brand a bit and appeal to younger generations using this slogan. Two years later they announced that Olds, as a brand, would no longer be on the market. They waited too long to change. Well, friends, it is not your parents' offering plate anymore, either. Will you wait too long to change?

Lyle Schaller wrote a brilliant book, *The New Context for Ministry*, dealing with the change in attitudes about charitable giving. In it, he plainly said, "This new face of American philanthropy is distinguished by an unprecedented level of competition for the charitable dollar. For well over 90 percent of all Christian congregations. . . . this means they will NOT be able to compete . . ." ([Nashville: Abingdon Press], 161).

By now I hope that you have come to the realization that competition is not a dirty word and that the church must engage in it. If so, then the rest of this book will prove useful. Maybe—just maybe—your church will be one of the 10 percent that learns how to compete and does so effectively.

QUESTIONS TO ASK

- In what ways have we experienced changes in the competitive environment for our church in our community?
- What are some of the ways our church has changed as the times have changed?

- If the young attorney had been a member of our church, would he have said that we wouldn't have known what to do with his gift?
- Specifically, what do you do differently today regarding financial stewardship that you were not doing ten years ago?

THINGS TO DO

- Invite the executive director of one of your community's first-rate nonprofits to come by and talk to your stewardship committee about how they do fund-raising and how they relate to their donors.

CHAPTER TWO

REASONS PEOPLE GIVE

W hen I first started working with nonprofits other than churches, I noticed one glaring difference. Nonprofits understood why people give. Not only did they understand why people give, but they structured all of their methods and appeals around such knowledge. Before I started working with them, I had only my church experience behind me, and I realized that neither I nor the churches had any idea how donors think or why they act the way they do.

What a novel idea. Actually trying to understand why people would want to give to you. We see this all the time. Grocery store owners have a very good idea of what makes people choose their grocery store and they adjust everything to appeal to the people their livelihood depends on. Wal-Mart may be the American company that understands best why people choose certain places to shop. Their rapid rise to the top of retailing shows that they understand their customers well. Nonprofits started studying a long time ago what caused a donor to choose one nonprofit over another, and as the number of nonprofits has grown, more and more have been applying what they have learned. Those who did it well are alive and well today. Those who ignored the evidence are no longer with us.

In one of my clergy seminars, I put up on a screen a laundry list of reasons people give. I then asked the pastors to choose which ones they felt were the number one, two, and three chief reasons people give. They started blurting out, "taxes, guilt, involvement . . ." No one was even close. Finally, a lady who had been sitting quietly in the back raised her hand and said, "Number one is a belief in the mission. Number two is a regard for staff leadership, and number three is fiscal responsibility." She was right. I was stunned. I asked her where she was a pastor and she sheepishly said, "I am not a pastor, but my pastor told me about this seminar and thought I might learn something. I am the executive director of Habitat for Humanity."

How revealing was that? The room was full of people who were all nonprofit leaders. A hundred of them were the heads of a church and one was the head of a secular nonprofit. The only one who understood why people gave was the one representing the secular organization. One of the most important things you can glean from this book is an understanding of why people give, and then you will begin to understand that the people in your pews are potential donors, not just members.

Jerold Panas's landmark book, *Mega Gifts,* was one of the first attempts to do in-depth research into the area of what motivates people to give. Almost annually since the book first came out in 1984, a number of other researchers have asked the question—why did you choose to make a gift? Their results have paralleled those Panas found early on. Panas discovered that for major donors three factors ranked extremely high. As stated before, they were (1) belief in the mission of the institution, (2) a high regard for staff leadership, and (3) the fiscal responsibility of the institution. Today nearly all nonprofits structure their fundraising around an understanding of these three reasons. They choose to do or not to do certain things depending on how they will motivate or discourage the giving of the donor. Only the church seems ignorant of the reasons people give.

A BELIEF IN THE MISSION

People want to make the world a better place to live. They want to believe that they can truly make a difference for the better. There is embedded in us, it seems, a desire to finish out our work on this earth with a sense that we amounted to something. To sum it up, people want to be a part of something that *changes lives.*

This is what nonprofits offer to do. People may work for a widget factory without feeling a strong sense of purpose or without being able to see how they make a difference in the world, so they give to a nonprofit to participate in what they would like to see happen. It is the nonprofit that helps them feed the hungry, clothe the naked, heal the sick, give hope to the hopeless, bring peace to the troubled, and in general make the world a better place to live. Nonprofits and churches only have one thing to sell—changed lives. When they do it well, they are supported, but when they do not do it well, they go out of business.

When I asked that young attorney why he was giving to the youth center instead of to his church, his answer could be summed up as follows: "The youth center showed me how they were changing lives with what they possessed and how they would change even more lives if they had more. The church has not shown me how it is performing its mission now, or how it plans to do it better if I choose to give them more money. I want to make a difference with what God has given me, and I do not see the church making much of a difference."

The supreme business guru of our time has been Peter Drucker. He wrote a great little book called *Managing the Nonprofit Organization*. In it he said, "A business has discharged its task when the customer buys the product, pays for it, and is satisfied with it. Government has discharged its function when its policies are effective. The nonprofit institution neither supplies goods, services, or controls. Its product is neither a pair of shoes nor an effective regulation.

Its product is a *changed human being*. The nonprofit institutions are human change agents. Their 'product' is a cured patient, a child that learns, a young man or woman grown into a self-respecting adult; a changed human life altogether" ([New York: HarperCollins, 1990], xiv).

In other words, what Drucker is saying is that just like people expect the shoe store to sell quality shoes at a good price, they expect the nonprofit to change lives. When a shoe store does a good job of selling quality shoes at a fair price, people keep buying shoes from that store. When a church consistently shows its constituency how lives are being improved through its ministry, then that church gets supported.

The best way to raise money for your church is simply to DO YOUR JOB! When people see others coming to your altar and falling on their knees, when they see families moving forward to unite their lives with you, when they hear testimonies of how a marriage was rejuvenated or an alcoholic rehabilitated, when they witness a group of young people singing of their love for Christ with sincere smiles on their faces, when they know deep in their own soul that they have moved closer to the cross through worship experiences—then they give.

I get frustrated reading newsletters of church after church that tell me how the men's group is going to have a breakfast on Saturday and the women are going to have a bazaar next Thursday and the youth will have a dance next

Friday after the ball game. Then, over in the corner, usually separated by a bold line so that it stands out, I see financial statistics, which usually indicate that a certain amount was needed and a lesser amount was received, and that there is a deficit of something, with a quote underneath, "God loves a cheerful giver."

When I see that I want to say, "What have I got to be cheerful about?" Did you show me one life story in this newsletter about how the church has been making our world better? Is there one life-changing story in the entire document? Do you really just exist so that men can have breakfast, women a bazaar, and youth can dance? What is it exactly that you want me to support?

There is not one nonprofit that Horizons works with that would send out a newsletter like that. Each and every communication tool they send out or put on a website contains one testimony after another. There are no financial statistics anywhere to be found. The entire communiqué is a collection of stories showing how they are doing exactly what people want them to do—make a difference and change lives.

I got a donor letter the other day from a large southern church. It was their main appeal letter for support for the upcoming year. What was their message about why they deserved the support of the people? We need 3 percent more than last year! That was it. The letter bragged about how the staff had done a great job of not spending much money the previous year, and if people will just come up with 3 percent more, they can get by once again and balance the budget. The summation of the entire letter was that we exist to balance a budget and here's how you can help us do it. This church is losing about forty members per year yet seems happy that they are managing to balance the budget.

Please hear me when I say that you are not in business to balance budgets or manage money. You are in business to change lives for the sake of the gospel of Jesus Christ—that is it. You have no other reason to exist. If you are not doing that, then get out of the way and let someone else have your spot. We are running out of time and losing our donor base by not doing our job. Move over and let someone else run your church and try to make a profit (make disciples).

The other day while watching television, I saw an infomercial for St. Jude Hospital in Memphis, Tennessee. This is the hospital Danny Thomas founded to work with very sick (with cancer usually) children. It is a massive hospital that treats thousands of children and employs thousands of people. I can only imagine what their yearly budget is to run this healing place.

I watched this infomercial for thirty minutes. Not one time did it say anything about how big their buildings were. Not one time did it mention what the CEO made. Not one time did it say what the utility bill runs. For thirty minutes it told me the story of one three-year-old child and how the hospital took that one child and over a period of many weeks helped this dangerously ill little boy go from being near death to having an energetic, vigorous life. I saw pictures of him in the hospital with tubes plugged into him and nurses gathered around him. I saw worried parents with a caring staff and doctors poring over X-rays. Finally, I saw a little boy on a swing set in his backyard, laughing and loving life. Not once did I think about budgets or numbers. I just saw a little boy getting well and I liked that. I want to support a place that makes three-year-old boys well. They showed me and told me the story of their mission and I believe in that mission. They got my support.

From the southern church who sent me the donor letter, I got a line item budget showing me that we pay $32,000 a year in utilities and $80,000 in conference obligations. They noted that more money is needed for next year and hoped I would raise my pledge.

Now, I was a pastor for twenty-four years and I know that the church changes the lives of many people. I was at the altar with many of them. I have been at the hospital with them and have gone to AA to support them. I have taken groups to prisons and to Haiti. I have listened to that young person share with me how Christ was shaping their life in one direction or another. I know the church is changing lives. But we are doing a real good job of keeping it a secret for some reason.

Recently I was visiting with a man who belongs to a church just outside Houston. The purpose of my call was to inquire about a possible gift to the church. Shortly after we began our conversation, he said to me, "I plan to give and to give substantially to the church, because the church saved my life." I encouraged him to go on and explain. "About two years ago my wife suddenly left me. I had no clue we were even having problems. We had two small children and I was just devastated. I went to a church I had never been to before and just sat in the back. One Sunday I got up enough courage to check in the register that I wanted someone to call me. The very next day the senior pastor did and I shared with him my pain and also that I was not a member of the church. He did not seem to mind where my membership was, but he sure was concerned for my well-being. He offered to connect me with one of their Stephen ministers [lay care team]. That person saved my life. He came to me and right off shared how a similar thing had happened to him. Over the next few weeks he helped me find hope again and to realize that though my wife had left me and my life had just changed dramatically, God had never left and he had a wonderful plan for the rest of my life."

I was moved by the story and asked the man if he had ever shared this with the church. He paused and then said, "No one has asked me to, but I would be glad to do that." I called the pastor and suggested that he immediately contact this man, hear his story, and find a way to use it on Sunday morning. This man is exactly the kind of customer that the church is most called to serve and a firsthand testimony like this tells our donors that we are doing what they are giving us money to do.

In one of my seminars, a pastor questioned if it would be appropriate to share how lives are being changed. He mentioned that much of that is confidential. Not if the person does the sharing or gives their permission. I am sure that St. Jude got permission to share about the three-year-old that was healed. In many of our evangelical churches, a person will share their testimony prior to being baptized. They are not forced. They are delighted to share what Christ is doing in their life. Most of our worship services would be greatly improved if five minutes of anything was replaced with five minutes of testimony, either video or live, each week. Our newsletters and websites would finally become effective if we would get all the announcements out and substitute one person's testimony of how Christ, through the church, changed his or her life.

When we do this, we will be appealing to the number one reason people give. We will be sharing with them how we are doing our mission and changing lives. When they see that we are affecting lives like the hospitals and youth centers and soup kitchens, THEN they will start giving to us like they give to the hospitals, youth centers, and soup kitchens.

REGARD FOR STAFF LEADERSHIP

Consistently ranking high on most donor surveys about why they chose to give where they did, is the regard the donor had for those who lead the organization. My experience has shown that this is becoming more and more important to church donors every year.

People realized a long time ago that it was not the Mayflower that sailed across the ocean to America; it was the pilgrims who did the sailing. It was not the bat that hit the home run to win the game; it was the batter. It was not the hospital that performed the operation to save your life; it was the surgeon. In the same manner, they have learned that the church building or program is not what is changing lives; it is the people leading that church and those programs that make the difference. When they have confidence in those people to perform, gifts follow. When they do not, those gifts go to people in whom they have confidence.

Early on in my ministry, a bishop asked me if I wanted to leave my assignment and go to another church. I told him that I was involved in a capital campaign and I thought my leaving would harm the church. He berated me rather severely for thinking too highly of myself and said, "People do not give to the pastor. They give to the church. I would not be moving the church, just you. It won't make any difference." At the time I assumed he was right, and had to admit that, frankly, often I did think too highly of myself.

What I have learned after working with over two hundred churches is that he was wrong. The person leading the flock makes a lot of difference in whether today's donor contributes as completely as they can. When they see a pastor who has a great vision and shows excellent skills in leadership, they will invest in that pastor's vision and trust in his or her skills to make the hopes of the donor come true.

The young attorney I talked about in the introduction did not have great confidence in the youth center, but he did have confidence in the executive director, who convinced him that the center could change lives if only they had more funds. The 1.5 million was given to that director, not to the center.

In recent years, we have seen a trend to move some very effective pastors in the middle of campaigns. I can bear witness to the devastating effect this has had on every single campaign. It was not that the congregation did not accept the new pastor, but they did not have enough confidence in him or her yet to make a significant gift. One man told me this past year, "I am pulling my hundred thousand for now. I want to see what sort of person we get and whether I believe he can deliver on our plans or not." What I knew was that we would not see that money for at least three years, and then only if the pastor had convinced this man and others that he could lead.

In every nonprofit with which I have ever worked, at the top of the job description for their executive director is fund-raiser. This is true in all colleges, hospitals, youth groups, children's groups, and other social service agencies. They know if they cannot raise funds, they cannot perform their mission. They are also keenly aware that the chief fund-raiser must be the person who can have the most influence on that mission—the CEO. The college president, the hospital administrator or chairman, the youth center executive director or whoever is perceived to be in charge must be the number one vision caster and fund-raiser for that vision. All nonprofits know this except the church.

The church actually brags about not having the senior pastor involved in finances. In the churches I have worked with in the last dozen years, over half of them have a senior pastor (CEO of the institution) who knows nothing regarding the donor base of the church. When I talk to the lay leadership of those churches, I find that they are actually proud of the fact that they have never had their minister involved with money. This attitude is 180 degrees from what it should be. The interesting thing I have noted is that in fast-growing denominational churches as well as non-denominational churches, the senior pastor ALWAYS has an excellent grasp of what is happening with his donor base.

One of the most dramatic examples of a pastor not knowing his donor base happened in a large suburban church that we worked with just a year ago. The pastor had been in place for eighteen months and our firm was going to conduct a capital campaign. We asked for a list of all the donors to the church, which is customary. This was sent to us by the church treasurer, because the pastor did not want anything to do with finances, and, frankly, the church thought that was a good idea. As we reviewed the list of the top ten contributors to the church, we saw that they gave about 38 percent of the total budget. It also became evident that not only did the pastor not know what these people were giving, he did not even know some of the people. Our consultant said, "People would come in to be recruited to help in the campaign and I found myself introducing them to their pastor. One man had given $500,000 the previous year and the preacher did not have a clue."

Now, would someone please explain to me how that attitude is helpful to the kingdom of God?

In 2004, a United Methodist bishop asked Horizons Stewardship to conduct a stewardship survey of all of his clergy (about 500). To encourage a good response to the survey, he even added a five dollar bill to each survey. Seventy-five percent were returned to us. The responses were anonymous. One of the questions dealt with whether the pastor knew the giving records of his or her members. We found that only about 27 percent knew what their members were giving. From those who did not know, it was more or less evenly split between those who were not allowed to know by the church leaders, and those pastors who chose not to know. In my opinion, that 73 percent are making a big mistake if they seriously want to improve financial stewardship in their congregations.

What happens when a pastor does not know? Lots of things and most of them are bad. First, when choosing leadership, the pastor often selects people whom he or she perceives to be good leaders and stewards, but they may just have big mouths. I have frequently seen finance committees where the chair and the majority of participants were nowhere close to leading the way in giving.

Once, out in California, I showed up to help a minister recruit a team that was to raise several million dollars to expand the church's educational complex. As I arrived that day, his treasurer gave me a list of donors that I had been seeking for some time, and the pastor gave me a list of those he felt should serve in this capital funding mission. I put the two lists side by side and immediately broke into a cold sweat. The man the pastor had chosen to lead the effort was an active participant in the church, but his total gifts the previous year amounted to $500. This man was not a giver, and now we would be asking him to lead an effort to help people give. I went down the pastor's list and found that not one single person he felt would be a good leader was in the top fifty donors to his church. We were about to make a crucial error. If we had moved forward with his list of leaders, it would have been like marching off to war with a group of pacifists. They might be good people, but they had never exemplified anything that showed that they could succeed in this task. We had two hours to find cochairs for all of our positions to make sure that a major donor was on every committee. Thank God we got it done and his campaign succeeded.

Second, it prevents the pastor from ever extending a personal thank-you to those who may have given generously. Understand, we are competing with one million nonprofits, all of whom readily thank their donors. The church stands alone, the one place where the CEO will seldom say thank-you for a gift. If I am competing for the hearts and pocketbooks of individuals and I know that I have six other people who are also competing for those same hearts and pocketbooks, I do not want to be the only one who takes that person for granted. I, at least, want my appreciation to be expressed as sincerely and as often as the others.

The other day my banker called to invite me to join him and a few other "customers" for a ball game in the bank's private suite. He said, "I would like you to be my guest as a way of expressing how much I appreciate your business." I went and had a wonderful time. He even tossed in a couple of hot dogs and all the diet soda I could drink. When I came to this town, there was only one bank. Now there are nine. My banker realizes that he must compete for my business now, and he is trying hard to do just that. Saying thanks is just one of the ways he is doing that.

Third, and most important, it denies the pastor insight into what is happening within a person's soul. Nothing is more revealing of what is happening inside people's hearts than what decisions they are making with their pocketbook. A famous evangelist once said, "The one thing standing between God and a person's heart is their wallet." I believe that is true. It is not foolproof, but it is one of the few indicators we have as to a person's relationship with Christ.

If pastors choose not to know how their members are doing in financial stewardship, I believe they are committing clergy malpractice. They are denying themselves a tool that could help diagnose a person's spiritual condition and that should be what all pastors are about. More than anything else, all pastors are to be in the soul-winning business.

Now, let me make one thing perfectly clear. Saving a person's soul, making disciples for Jesus Christ, and building the kingdom of God is the business we are in. We are in no other business. The involvement of our pastors and staff with money is, and should only be, done to advance the reason we are in business. The love of material things is our greatest sin (our golden calf) and our pastors and staff are called to break it down.

To sum up, if we keep our church staff and pastors apart from the intimate details of what is happening financially, we lose the ability to take advantage of the second most motivating factor of why people give, and we lose a critical tool that can be used to save souls.

FISCAL STABILITY OF THE INSTITUTION

People do not give to sinking ships. They give to ships that are sailing strong and give every indication of reaching their destination. When people invest in nonprofits, they do not want to waste their investment. In recent years, the use of charitable dollars has come under heavy scrutiny. The Red Cross and United Way have been contending with scandals over how donations are used. Lawsuits abound where donors are suing colleges and hospitals over not using a donation appropriately. Charitable institutions today are being held to a different standard than even a few years ago. Donors feel the same way about the church. More than ever they are holding the church accountable for wise use of funds and looking for solid performance with the funds already given. We must be very careful in the messages we send out, to ensure that they don't convey that we are not fiscally sound, when oftentimes we are.

The church is the only nonprofit I know of that seems to believe that the more you cry that you are sinking, the more people will give to you. The exact opposite is true. No nonprofit I know of would ever send out a donor letter stating that they are running a horrible deficit and they just want the donors to help balance the budget. They know that such a letter actually discourages giving rather than motivates it. A nonprofit board will deal with budget matters in a board meeting but never publicize such to its donor base. The church goes out of its way to do just that.

Most finance committees are anxious to put giving statistics in the bulletin even though they know that for eleven months of the year they will be showing a deficit. They do it believing that if people think things are bad, they will give more than if they think things are going well. They think crying wolf is a good idea. I actually get more calls in my office from finance chairpersons worried that they are now running a surplus than from those who are concerned about running a deficit. The problem: they do not want the congregation to know things are going well, assuming that they will then quit giving. The theory in these churches is if we can say we are going broke, people will give us more than if we tell them we are changing lives. In fact, the exact opposite is true.

In the nonprofit world, two institutions continue to outperform most of the others. The Salvation Army continues to get more donations each year than any social service agency or group. Harvard University leads all universities in endowment-giving year after year. Do they send out a message that they are dying on the vine and must have one more contribution to stay afloat? No, they say, "We took your money last year and we did great things with it. If you will give us more, we will do more great things." And people give and give to them. People want results and these institutions give positive results!

The great advice from our finance committees to our preachers is, "Get up there Sunday and tell them how bad it is, Preacher. Tell them that if they do not give, we are going to lay off staff and cut off the air-conditioning on Sunday morning. Tell them we won't be able to last much longer before the bank comes and gets us. That will really make them give, Preacher." We got it backwards again.

If you are on the finance committee of your church, I hope you will take this chapter to your next meeting, and when they whip out the line item budget to start trimming things because you are once again running behind, stop them and say, "Hey, the top three reasons people give are (1) belief in the mission, (2) regard for staff leadership, and (3) fiscal responsibility. Instead of just cutting our budget, could we review how well we tell our donors about how we do our job of changing lives? Could we review how well we utilize our staff and pastor when it comes to relating to our donors? Could we look to see if we are sending signals that we are fiscally sound or fiscally unsound? It may be that if we could fix these three areas, we would not have to cut the budget again."

After the meeting is over, let me know how it went.

QUESTIONS TO ASK

- In what ways are we specifically sharing testimonies of how we fulfill our mission as a church?
- Have we ever asked our pastor to be sure and involve himself or herself with our key supporters?

• Do we inadvertently do things that communicate that we are not fiscally sound, like putting giving records in the bulletin or newsletter?

THINGS TO DO

• Get someone from the church to find fifty-two testimonies for use each week of the year in either worship or in your newsletter. This seems to work much better if a staffperson has it as a specific responsibility. Once you begin the process, you will find that people all over the church will suggest testimonies from people they know or from experiences they have had.

• Go back five years and chart what percentage of income comes in each month. Then when you report how giving is going, you can do so honestly by reporting what has come in as compared to what the church's income history has been. Instead of reading, "We are halfway through the year and yet we have only received 42 percent of our expected income," the report will say, "we are halfway through the year and generally our church has received 42 percent of its income to date. So far we are right on track at 42 percent in." This is honest and it does not give the false impression that you are in fiscal distress.

CHAPTER THREE

ALL MEMBERS ARE NOT EQUAL

One of the most ridiculous but oft-heard expressions in a church is that all members should be treated equally. Yet, I have never seen a church truly treat all its members equally except when it comes to fund-raising.

If Jane has cancer and has been told she has only a few weeks to live, should the pastor treat Jane equal to all other members? If Sally moves to town and the pastor understands that she used to sing with the Metropolitan Opera in New York, should he treat her exactly like all other members? If John has just been told he is going to be laid off at his job, should he be treated equal to all other members? Of course not! This seems so simple and so silly, doesn't it? Yet, if I add to the above that Mary has been promoted to CEO of MegaCorp, a publicly traded company and earns a seven-figure salary, should she be treated exactly like all other members?

Let me suggest that all of these people should be given special treatment from the pastor, because the pastor is concerned about the souls of all of them. As pastors, we know that when people are near death, they have a number of issues about life everlasting that other members do not have, and they have need for the special attention of their pastor. When one is gifted with extraordinary talent, one has the choice of using it for God's purposes or for some other purpose. As pastors, we know that we need to share with those individuals how to use that talent for the Lord. When a person loses his or her job, we know that despair can easily set in and destroy a life or a family. We give special attention to help that person go through deep waters. But we often pretend that money is not to be addressed or paid attention to because surely we wouldn't think money could corrupt someone or cause them to lose their way? From a study of the Scriptures, it would appear that Christ had great concern for the wealthy. It was not that he wanted their money, but he knew how easily money could pull them away from their heavenly Father.

Do I hear protest from the masses? Yes, I do. The protest comes from the multitudes in the pews who like to complain that the preacher only cares for the rich people. This is a wonderful complaint to make because rich people are a real minority in most churches, and so it is easy for one to get cohorts to join in the protest. Go back and read the Zacchaeus story in Luke 19:1-10. It notes that Zacchaeus was a *rich* man. Then it says that Jesus said, "I *must* stay at your house" (v. 5, emphasis added). And the people grumbled. He did not say that he must stay at the home of a sick person or a middle-class person, but for whatever reason Jesus felt that there was a divine necessity to go to this rich person's home. By the time he left the home, Jesus had two gifts from Zacchaeus: (1) one-half of his net worth and (2) his soul. I believe that the soul was the greatest gift Jesus walked away with, but the financial gift was intricately tied to it. Indeed, if Zacchaeus could not have given his money, it probably would have shown Jesus that he did not have his soul.

Now, of course, Jesus often chose a sick person or a lame person or a poor person to give special attention to. We all know those stories and they show important things about the character of Jesus. But at other times, the ones with whom he spent special time were the rich. Are we not called to do the same? With whom was Jesus more concerned about being able to enter the Kingdom of Heaven . . . the rich or the poor?

The argument that I hope you hear being made is that the rich need the attention of their pastor to know how to handle the burden of money. They need help with giving to save their souls. Just as it would be clergy malpractice to not visit someone who was dying and needed close and intimate prayer, it is also clergy malpractice to ignore a member who is being pulled into hell by the weight of his wallet. But the multitudes have not changed one bit since Jesus' day. They will still grumble when the sinful minority gets the attention of the chief shepherd. Sometimes we have to remember that we are called by a higher power than the grumblers.

Now let's address another area where nearly all of our churches are guilty of treating members equally. This is with the infamous finance letter. We have all gotten them, written by either the pastor or the chairperson of finance, making us aware that the church is behind on its finances and encouraging us to give a bit more as the year comes to a close. It is a disgusting and usually ineffective letter and it is mailed to 100 percent of the membership with the most helpful greeting of "dear member." Why would we ever believe that such an instrument would be helpful? No nonprofit that I have ever been acquainted with would send all of its donors the same communiqué.

Nonprofits that know they must do a good job of communicating to stay alive do not treat their donors equally. My college is a good example of this.

My father, my son, and I attended the same college. Dad graduated in 1949. I was in the class of 1973 and my son finished in 1999. My dad is a retired business executive, I am in my mid-fifties with thirty years in ministry, and my son is twenty-eight, recently married and starting a career. We share a last name, but other than that we are very different. Our college is well aware that the class of 1949 needs a different style of communication than the class of

1999. Imagine that! They guessed that my dad, who went through World War II and then successfully ran several companies and raised three children before retiring, might think differently about giving than his grandson, who has spent about six years in the workforce and has his children's college educations and his own retirement still ahead of him.

From time to time, we get together and compare what the college is sending us and how they are communicating with us. We get different pieces of mail dealing with different topics. My son is getting mail encouraging him to get involved in the annual fund and to start being a contributing alumnus of some sort. My mail is encouraging me to move my giving to a higher level, because I have been a contributor for a number of years, and my dad is getting considerable correspondence about estate giving. It is very targeted for a specific audience. Can we not be that smart?

I am a tither to my church on a very regular and systematic basis. In addition to that, I frequently contribute for extra needs that my church might encounter during the year. Last year, I got a letter just like everyone else asking me to consider tithing and giving a bit more as the year came to a close. I resented it. Why was I being prodded to give more when that was what I was already doing? Where was my thank-you letter for what I was doing for the church? It did not motivate me to give more—it frustrated me.

At the same time that I got my letter, I know that 40 percent of the people who belong to our church but do not give got the same letter. They are giving ZERO and the letter asks them to consider giving a tithe or giving an increase. Well, now, I am sure that as soon as they read that letter, they will start pulling 10 percent right off the top of the next paycheck. NOT! They will look at the letter and think, "Let's double what we are doing. Now, what is two times zero? Oh, it is ZERO!" There is nothing about that letter that is going to move them one bit. However, if they had gotten a special note with their name on it and been asked to consider giving five dollars a week, some might have gotten on board. Then you could have thanked them for that and later moved them to ten dollars.

We need to end this practice of believing that it is best if we treat members equally. Those who are giving exemplary leadership need to be getting thank-you communications. Those who have been giving for a while but have never moved up to the tithe need help to get there. Those who have never given just need to be affirmed if they will do something—anything. Let's take another lesson from the nonprofits and target-market in our approach.

You can choose exactly how you want to divide up your congregation for your mailing. There are some obvious divisions. One way is to divide your congregation up by generations. Almost all nonprofits know that what motivates a person of the World War II generation is not what motivates a Baby Boomer or a Gen Xer.

They understand that the WW II group is very loyal to institutions. They are very comfortable believing in big government and big church. If the President said it is so, then it is so, and if the church says they need something, that is all they need to know.

The Baby Boomers have gone through Vietnam, Watergate, and Iraq. They are not nearly as trusting in leadership as their parents are. Just because the church says to do something does not necessarily make it right. They will ask questions and hold institutions accountable to perform.

Gen Xers have lost confidence in almost everything they cannot see, hear, and touch themselves. They are highly skeptical and do not hold big institutions in nearly as high regard as they do small, local groups.

So, what does that tell me? It tells me that I can use language with my father that says the church needs you to give something and we need it by this time frame. That is all. No further explanation needed or wanted. If the church says so, then it is so.

For the Baby Boomer, you had better be ready to justify the need with some facts, to make them aware of how sound an investment it is compared to other giving opportunities they may have. You will have to put your case up front to allow comparison.

For Gen Xers, you had better provide time for them to actually come and see what you need, and you need to be be ready to explain exactly why you need it and how it will benefit those whom they can readily see and understand.

Don't even waste the paper on sending a WW II letter to a Gen Xer.

The other logical division, depending on the type of letter you are doing, is by giving levels. You should send a solicitation letter to a tither that is different from the letter sent to a member who has not given anything all year. All in all, I used to divide my congregation up by at least four groups: tither, consistent giver, one who gives something, and no gift at all. I know that it will take an hour or so of extra time to write four letters instead of one, but it will probably double your response—not bad for one hour's work!

QUESTIONS TO ASK

- Are we sending out the same correspondence to all of our donors?
- If we were to start sending out mail depending upon age or giving history, how many different mailings should we have?
- Do we use multimedia (preferred by younger donors) as well as traditional mail?

THINGS TO DO

- Instead of just mailing the message to your members, try dividing up your church into giving types (tithers, solid givers, never give, and so on) and having these persons over for an evening at the pastor's home, where a particular message can be conveyed for that particular group.

• Produce two or three different DVDs to mail into particular homes, where you share the vision and ask for support.

• Insist that the pastor have a special time (lunch or home visit) with the top ten donors to your church just to listen to them and hear their hopes and dreams for the church. Be sure he or she shares those ideas that may be on the table for the future to gauge the donors' receptivity. You are not treating these people any differently than you would be treating choir members whom you might meet with to discuss ways music may be used in the future. A smart pastor would make a few visits to those who would be doing the heavy lifting (choir members) to test their support before just bringing up a change. The same needs to be done with those who will be carrying the heaviest load financially. It is not a requirement, but it is smart!

CHAPTER FOUR

THE PASTOR *MUST* BE A FUND-RAISER

In remembering the story of Zacchaeus, I like to focus on the word *must*. Jesus said that he *must* go to the home of this rich man. As noted earlier in chapter 3, it turned out to be a pretty good visit, with Jesus walking away with the man's soul, plus a gift of one-half of the rich man's net worth. Now, one can suppose that Zacchaeus just volunteered such gifts, but I doubt it. My guess is that somewhere in the visit Jesus made what is referred to in fund-raising as an *Ask*. Zacchaeus's offer was his response to the Ask. Though we do not know for certain whether or not Jesus made such an Ask, we do know that Jesus went to Zacchaeus's home as part of a larger plan. It was no accident that Jesus wound up there. He intended to visit that home that day.

Pastors are the CEOs of their congregations. No single person is more responsible for what goes on in his or her church than the lead pastor. No one is more able to shape the future than the lead pastor. No one has more communication with the congregation than the lead pastor. No one has more ability to raise funds on behalf of the church than the lead pastor. Yet, very few of our pastors accept the responsibility to raise funds for the organization they lead.

At Horizons, we are often called upon by nonprofits to help them find a new executive director or president to run their organizations. We sit down with the board and review the qualifications they are looking for. At the top of the list every single time is "ability to raise funds." Yes, he or she certainly must have great affection for the work of that particular organization, but the number one attribute is still fund-raiser. Why? Because it does not matter how much you want to heal the sick, or care for young people, or educate the masses, you will fail if you do not have the funds to operate.

In the church, sadly enough, it is frequently the opposite. I have worked with many churches that actually brag that their pastor is not privy to finances. Oh, they will let him or her sit in on finance committee meetings and sometimes tell him or her to cry on Sunday morning for a larger offering, but they will not let the pastor know what people give or allow the pastor to ask someone for a gift. For some reason they feel that this separation makes the pastor more holy. What it does is make him or her far less effective and tends to make money a bigger issue in the church than ministry.

The most important person in terms of raising money for a university is the university president. He or she is the sole person who can represent the vision to the donor and communicate the confidence that a gift will be used to fulfill that vision. When the president does so, no one ever accuses him or her of not caring about educating students. The president knows that those dollars are necessary to educate those very students.

The most important person in terms of raising money for a hospital is the chairperson of the board or the president of the hospital. This person alone can represent the need to the donor in such a way that if the donor chooses to make the gift, the donor knows that individual has the authority to ensure that the gift will go directly to fulfill that need. Anyone else would have to tell the donor that they would have to check with their director first. No one accuses the chairperson of not caring about sick people. They know that for the sick to get better, equipment and facilities must be made available and those cost money.

Why do we not look at the CEOs of our churches the same way? The church is a nonprofit organization that depends upon people giving money to it for its work to be done. Yet, we think that somehow this just happens on its own. More and more donors are expecting the pastors of churches to represent their organization to them just like the heads of other nonprofits represent their respective organizations. When pastors do not do it, the church loses out.

Where did we get the idea that it was somehow good for pastors to not know the giving of their members? Would you want the president of your college to tell you that he or she was not aware of who gave what to the college? Would you want the executive director of a nonprofit board to which you belonged to tell you that he or she did not want to know the donors to your nonprofit? Of course not! We would not want this because we know it would do irreparable harm to our college or to our beloved nonprofit. Why, then, do we not encourage our pastors to show such leadership?

The answer is found, once again, in the story of Zacchaeus. It is because the people grumble. And why do the people grumble? Is it because they believe that knowing will somehow harm the church? Is it that they believe people will decide to give less when they know the pastor knows? Is it because they believe that if the pastor knows, the church will somehow not fulfill its mission? No. It is because most of them are not giving as they know the Bible commands, and they do not want light shed on that fact. It is the same reason that so few pastors are invited to a New Year's Eve party or out to the casino on Friday night. The people involved are sinning, and they would just as soon keep the pastor in the dark about it as long as they can. That is why they grumble. It has nothing to do with the church. It has everything to do with their own sin.

I love it when I hear people say such things as "giving should be just between the giver and God." That is malarkey. It is never just between the giver and God and never has been. Now, I guess if you took your money out in the woods and said, "God, I am going to throw this up to you, take all you want," that might be just between you and God. But to give in just about any other way involves a lot of people. When you give, someone collects the money. Someone else counts it and another records it in the church's records. If you itemize your tax return, then someone else probably puts the amount you gave in the right box. If you get a loan, they will ask to see your tax return and an entire bank board will see what you gave. In reality, for most of us, ten to twenty people will have access to information about what we choose to give. This is not about the donor and God. It is about the donor and the pastor and the fact that many do not want the one who runs their church to know that they support it so poorly.

A pastor knowing what people give will help in countless ways. First (though not necessarily most important), it will help the pastor raise more money. For a person to be able to make a gift, they must have two things—the capability and the will. Knowing what someone gives will not always tell you about capability, but it *will* tell you about will. Knowing what someone gives will tell you more about what they are committed to than anything else. As the Bible noted, treasure and heart go together. If you need to raise some funds for a much-needed addition and you need a lead donor, the best place to look is at your current lead donors. They obviously have the will and if they also have the capability, then you have a good chance of getting the gift.

Second, knowing what people give will help you determine the effectiveness of church programs. There are not many indicators available to us on what is happening inside one's heart, but giving is a good one. When we first launched a major, new initiative in Bible study at one of my last churches, I took the fifteen people who signed up and wrote down what they were currently giving to the church. When we finished that thirty week endeavor, I again looked at what they were giving and saw a dramatic increase. That told me the Bible study program was changing lives and we needed to expand it. Nothing could have told me that like the amount people were giving.

Third, knowing what members give will let you give thanks for the gift. Most nonprofits require their leaders to offer a thank-you to all donors within one week. They do it because they know that it is vital to getting the next gift. The church is notorious for not saying thank-you to its donors. We will have people extend gifts of tens of thousands of dollars and never so much as get a thank-you card from the pastor. The reason? The pastor does not know it was given. He or she has no access to the giving records. I find this a tragedy. Someone could give the gift of a lifetime and then later pass by the pastor in the grocery store aisle and no mention of the gift would ever be made. Could the donor perhaps get the feeling that the pastor does not care or was just callous and rude? Sure they could. We must get in the habit each week of extending thanks to our members. Those with whom we are competing are certainly doing it.

Fourth, knowing what members give will help you capture the real gift: their soul. I am convinced that Jesus went to Zacchaeus's house to get his soul, not his money. But when Jesus heard of the gift of money, he knew he had Zacchaeus's soul.

I often hear pastors say, "I have no idea what someone makes or what they could give." That is just not true. We are not so dumb as to think that the CEO of a major corporation has the same income as a schoolteacher. We know that the person who owns a string of businesses throughout the state is probably making a bit more than the letter carrier. We know that the man who has ten thousand acres under plow may be in a different tax bracket than the firefighter. We see certain members living in huge mansions and others with two luxury cars in the driveway. There are lots of ways we gather knowledge of the material ability of people. When you see the CEO giving less than the schoolteacher or the bank president giving less than the police officer, it should be a clue about what is going on in their respective hearts. Our job at that point is to say with Jesus, "I *must* go to your house," not for money, but to inquire about the condition of your soul. Let's not fool ourselves. We often know that individuals have far more capability than what we see in the offering plate. We get a glimpse into where their treasure and heart are. If it is not with God, then we must help them remove that which stands between them and salvation.

Well, what about a pastor who gets this knowledge and abuses it? I know this happens on occasion. Pastors make mistakes, and they can also exercise bad judgment. Teachers, bankers, legislators, and police officers also sometimes make mistakes. However, when a police officer is caught stealing, you do not remove all police from the street, you discipline the guilty officer. When a teacher slaps a child, you do not stop all teachers from interacting with children, you discipline that irresponsible teacher. We should not tolerate a pastor who abuses confidential matters, whether it is about finances or a marriage. That pastor must be disciplined appropriately, but we should not punish all future pastors, or the church for that matter, by making rules that hamper pastors' ability to do their jobs effectively.

In summary, I can find no good reason for a pastor not to know other than to keep the sinners from grumbling. Surely we would not want them to be the ones who dictate our ministry.

Now let me get to the area that absolutely scares about 90 percent of pastors to death—ASKING for MONEY! This is hard for me to understand, but certainly true, that most preachers would rather drink a bucket of castor oil than go to a member and ask for funds to accomplish the work of the Lord. Why is that?

My guess is that we are afraid of rejection. Some pastors think that asking for money is sales, and a lot of pastors do not like sales. My wife once told me what she remembers of having to sell Girl Scout cookies. She would go up to a door, shaking and trembling, and say, "Hi, you don't want to buy any cookies, do you?" I think most of our pastors would approach members in much the same way. At least when they turned us down, they would be confirming what we already believed and we would not be so disappointed.

I do not look at asking for money as sales. I always look at it as evangelism. When I ask someone to give money for the work of the kingdom, I am doing nothing more than inviting them to be a part of what I so passionately believe to be the best place for their money and their life. I am asking them to join me in something that changed my life and that I believe has the power to change the lives of countless others. If we truly believe that Jesus Christ, through the church, can change the world, why would we not want to invite everyone we care anything about to be a part of it?

A dear friend of mine came to see me several years ago. She sat down in my office and began to tell me how much she loved a particular church camp and what that camp had done for her life. She explained that she had joined the board of the camp and had a vision of where the camp should go and what it could be. She was as passionate about this place as anyone could be. There was something contagious about her joy. Then she said, "Clif, I am giving five thousand dollars to the camp to move our plan forward, and I need you to join me. Would you consider making a five-thousand-dollar gift as well?" Then she shut up and just waited for my answer. I agreed to do as she asked.

I frequently think over that solicitation and why I responded positively to it when I have rejected so many others. You see, I knew of this camp, but I was not a frequent visitor and I had never had any particular life-changing event happen to me there. It did not occupy a large place in my heart. I agreed to the gift because of my relationship with this woman, who believed in it so passionately. I believed in what she wanted to do. I loved her vision for the place. In the end, I wanted to be a small part of what I perceived was going to make a real difference in people's lives. I believed this because of the confidence I had in my friend. In a real way, though I was making a check out to the camp, I was really making the gift to my friend.

The rule in fund-raising is that people give to people and not to programs. People know that programs are just words on paper until others take them and put those words into action. Only then do lives get changed. So, though I may like a certain program or idea, I do not give to it without having supreme confidence in the people who are going to be in charge of carrying it out. A CEO or board member is always preferable to a volunteer to make this communication because he or she has the power to carry out the vision. In the church, this means the pastor is the absolute best one to share the vision and to ask for support for it. I could support the camp without being asked to, but I can easily tell you that I would not have supported it as strongly as I did if I had not been asked to. I can also just wander into some church and become active in it, but I am more likely to do so if I am asked. I could have just decided to go to Rotary Club, but I never did until I was asked. My wife may have married me anyway, but I definitely did not know that until I asked. In each of the above cases, it could be said that sales was involved. I prefer to see it as having more to do with relationships than sales. People are being asked to enter into a new relationship or partnership when you ask them for money. You want them to join you in something you believe is vitally important.

A few years ago, I was in a room with the senior pastor of one of the largest churches in America. With us was one of his key laypeople. The pastor started to talk about his vision for the church. He talked about how many hundreds of children would use a center he hoped to build, and then he began to speak about the whole project, which would culminate with a sanctuary and meeting room that would seat thousands. As he spoke, he sort of trembled in anticipation of what it was going to mean to him. At each point on his verbal journey around the project, he would pause to speak of people who were not yet there who would come, and how many of those families were in homes without Christ. Then he paused, looked at me, and said, "I believe that not only can we lay a foundation to change thousands of lives right here in this place, but we can teach thousands of other churches all over America to do the same thing right where they are planted, to reach not thousands, but millions. I truly do believe that, if we can just succeed in this campaign." When he finished, I was ready to sign up to make the vision a reality. We took a break and the layperson came over to me and said, "Compelling, isn't it?" I just nodded. "Last week he asked me to lead this off with one million dollars. I told him I would not do that. I want to be in this for two million. I wouldn't miss this for the world."

I guess some people would call the pastor's pitch sales, but I call it great preaching in the spirit of those such as Joel, Isaiah, Paul, Peter, John Wesley, and Martin Luther King. Your pitch is nothing more than what you truly believe can be IF we succeed in this campaign.

So, how do you ask? Let me go back to the marriage proposal as an example. When I asked my wife to marry me, I did not just blunder over and say to her, "You want to marry me or not?" I told her how much I loved her and how committed I was to her. I said that I thought we could be very happy together. I shared what our relationship to date had meant to me, and, finally, I asked her to join me in marriage. Then I shut up and waited for her answer.

Asking for money (or for people to join you in something) is very much like a proposal. You first share with them how passionate you feel and how committed you are. (Note: You cannot ask someone to give if you have not already done so with a proportionate commitment). Then you ask them as specifically as you can. If you hope they will give five thousand dollars, then say so. If it is one million dollars, then say so. When I asked my wife to marry me, I did not say, "I was sort of wondering if we could maybe spend our nights together, like forever or something, or at least a lot of nights and a lot of time, and maybe weekends and some holidays, unless you are already obligated for some holidays, which of course I would understand and could work through it. I mean, gee, what do you think?" I just said, "Will you marry me?" She said *yes* to that question. I am not sure what answer I would have gotten to the previous one.

If there is one thing donors have consistently told me, it is to tell them exactly what I want to do and exactly what I need them to do. All of this should take about five to ten minutes, by the way.

The biggest problem a lot of pastors have is shutting up and getting the answer. They are so nervous that they go on and on and on, never giving the donor a chance to respond. You will get one of three answers.

One, they will say *yes*. In which case, you say *thank you* and let them know you will be confirming with them in a letter. You might even want to say *thank you* five or six or a dozen more times!

Two, they will say they want to talk to an advisor. In this case, you reply that you certainly understand and would expect that. Ask them if they know when they might have an answer for you, and do not be afraid to share what deadlines you have for responses. Again, say thank you several times.

Three, they will say *no*. In this case, ask them what level of gift they might be willing to consider. Let them pick where they feel comfortable. Once they do so, say *thanks* again and again. Chances are, they will pick a level higher than you would have picked for them.

If they reject you totally, tell them that you hoped they did not mind being asked, and that you felt comfortable in visiting with them and believed they would understand your passion and commitment for the project. Thank them for giving you the chance to share what obviously means so much to you. Again, remember that you have asked them to join you in something you love and that you felt they would love it too. That is a compliment, not an intrusion.

Now, if you are convinced that asking is something you should do on behalf of the kingdom, let me share with you some of the ground rules to make you more successful.

In making an Ask to someone with whom you have a good chance of being successful, these are the important things to consider beforehand: if the right person is asking the right person, at the right time, for the right amount, then you will succeed in getting the gift. Let me break it down for you.

The right person (to do the asking)—I mentioned earlier that when it comes to the church, generally the pastor is the right person to do the asking. This is because he or she has the ability to speak best on how the gift will be used and what can be accomplished with it in the institution (church) they run. It is also true that the pastor is usually the right one because they have a relationship with the potential donor, so both parties will be comfortable in the conversation. There are times, however, when another person is better than the pastor because of a long-standing trust that has been established. If another person makes the Ask, it is imperative that that person have a strong commitment to the project and have already made his or her exemplary commitment to it. Sometimes it is helpful if this person is accompanied by the pastor. Both have strong commitments to the project, but one has the relationship and the other has the expertise to answer questions or to give assurances of what will occur with the gift. In talking to one person or to a couple, I would never have more than two people go along for the Ask. You do not want to overwhelm the donor.

Place is important in making a call like this. My first preference is to go to a home or to a private office. Because of the sensitive nature of the call, you want to try and be in a place that assures privacy. Lunches and dinners are great for fellowship but do not usually make good settings to make a request for money. Also, do not have someone come to you unless there are no other options. You are the one asking for something and you should not start out by asking them to take their time to come to you.

The right person (to be asked)—To be a major donor, a person must have capability and will. Far too often I find pastors who do not check both categories before they make assumptions on what someone might give. Capability is certainly a subjective call and is assessed by pastors in various ways. We are often privileged to hear from members that they have a certain capability because of an inheritance they received, a company they sold, or a stock they received. Those who have ears, let them hear! Other times we are just aware of the position a person holds in a company, which surely guarantees them an income that is much higher than average. Sometimes it is announced in the paper that a company went public and what key officers are likely to make on day one of an IPO. Seldom do we know everything, but there are numerous ways we can make judgments on capability.

This is only where it starts, however. We must then ask ourselves the question, "Do they love us? Is there anything in this person's history that would lead me to believe that they would WANT to give to us?" The best place to look is their participation. What are they giving now? How often are they in worship? Do you see signs of discipleship and loyalty in their life? If you do, then you have a wonderful candidate to talk to about using that which he or she *has* to advance that which they obviously *love*. If you do not see any of these signs, I do not care if their name is all over the *Forbes* 400 list, they are not likely to make a significant contribution to your church. Why? Because they care about other things more than the church and that is where their money will go.

Just remember, *capability* and *will* must go together in determining if you are asking the right person.

The right time—In my second year of full-time pastoral ministry, I found myself involved in a project to relocate our church. We needed to get some early financial support, but I was clueless as to where to go and how to do it. I went to see the chairperson of our building project, who also happened to be a banker in the community. I told him my dilemma. He told me that I was the right person to go and make the visits, and he also told me whom I should see first.

When he told me the name of the man I should see before anyone else, I became a bit shaky. This old man was a big-time farmer whose family had been a part of the church for decades. He did not come to church a great deal, but he was one of our most faithful donors. He was also known to have a very independent streak, and rumor was he had eaten a couple of preachers in his day. As I shook in the banker's office, I said, "What should I ask him for?" He quickly said, "Well, to my knowledge no one has ever given ten thousand dollars at one time to this church. We need $100,000 to buy this property and that would be 10 percent of it. I would ask him for ten thousand dollars." At that time, my yearly salary was only $9,500. Ten thousand would be a whole lot of money. I replied, "OK, I will go do it in the morning." He looked at me and said, "Don't even think about going any time other than 1:30 in the afternoon." I was bewildered. He went on, "In the mornings, he is in the fields, until around noon. He comes in and eats lunch and then for one hour he watches *All My Children* [the soap opera]. It ends at 1:30. He will be in a good mood for about a half hour, until he goes back out again. You get there at 1:30 and be gone by 2:00."

Well, the magnitude of my fright went up about tenfold, but I did as my banker friend told me. I got there at 1:31 and found a very surprised old farmer at the door. I went in and told him what we were doing and that we needed his help. I can still remember when he cut me off with, "Cut to the chase, preacher. How much do you want from me?" I said, "I need ten thousand dollars." I think I may have passed out. He stuck out his lower lip a bit, squeezed his eyebrows together, and said, "Do you want a check now or can I get it to you Sunday morning?" I was gone by 2:00.

I have remembered the lessons learned through that ever since and used them subsequently to ask for over three million dollars from other donors. Do your research to determine if a particular time is better than another. What is going on in someone's life? Do they have time to concentrate on what you are asking them? Are office hours better or should you go to their home? Is it better to find a time when the spouse is there or not? Have they just sold a business or come into an inheritance where others are going to be getting in line to make an Ask? Doing a bit of homework can pay big dividends.

The right amount—This is critical. The biggest mistake you can make is asking for too low an amount. If the potential donor has million-dollar capability and you ask for ten thousand dollars, you are going to get it quicker than you can blink, but you will have shortchanged the church $990,000. You also will have short-changed the blessing for the donor by keeping them from being as instrumental as they could have been. Now, you could argue that they could still give a million dollars, and you would be right, but the fact is that all you told them you needed was ten thousand dollars and that is all you are likely to receive. They will still probably give away the remainder, just not to the church.

Determining potential is not an exact science, but it is not that difficult either. Look at what you know. Does the potential donor play professional baseball where the average salary is over a million dollars? I know you probably don't have any pro players in your church, but I hope you do see what I am saying. We really can make some suppositions about incomes and giving potentials. Are they heads of large corporations? Do they have lucrative medical or legal practices? Do they live in a subdivision where the average home sells for mega dollars? Have they communicated to you that they have recently inherited large sums of money? Have they given an extraordinary gift to the church before or did they make a large gift to another nonprofit? These are all questions we can review when determining what is the right amount to ask for. Speaking with other trusted people in the church can also be helpful, as it was to me with my first Ask.

We often fear asking for too much. I have found that people are seldom offended when this occurs. In fact, when my requests have been high, the response is generally, "I am flattered that you think I could do that, but that is over my head." I come back and simply ask, "What amount do you believe would be right?" What they tell me I am certain is far more than they would have done had I not asked.

All gifts, of course, depend upon the needs of the church and the project presented. You cannot ask someone to give one million dollars to a project that costs less than that. Generally, major donors want to help raise other gifts and they understand the need to give 10 to 20 percent of a project, but they do not want to be asked to do it all, while others do nothing.

Don't worry about not being a professional. Your people do not want to hear from a professional fund-raiser. They want to hear a vision and dream from their pastor. They want to know from *you* what they can do to help the dream become reality. They want to be servants of the same God you represent, and they need you to lead them. I know you feel vulnerable, but pick up your staff and go out there and do it on behalf of the God who calls you and promised to be with you. If he can part the Red Sea and defeat Pharaoh's army, then he just might help you raise some money for the kingdom.

QUESTIONS TO ASK

- Is it right to compare our pastor to the president of a college or head of a hospital? Is he or she really the CEO of our nonprofit?
- Why do you think some people do not want the pastor to know what they give?
- Have you ever used the phrase, "Giving is between the giver and God"? Do you believe that is true?
- Have you ever seen people give of themselves and been motivated by their sacrifice or commitment?
- If our pastor does not know the giving of our members, how can he or she be expected to thank people for extraordinary generosity? Do you believe that thanks would be appreciated?

THINGS TO DO

- Go to a nearby college or large hospital and seek out their vice president for advancement or the director of development and ask how they do major gift solicitation.

- In many communities, there are chapters of the Association of Fund-raising Professionals. These chapters host monthly meetings where fund-raising is taught. Many chapters have also partnered with local colleges to offer a certificate program in fund-raising. This is a four-session class that can be very instructive for pastors and lay finance leaders.

CHAPTER FIVE

THE THREE POCKETS OF GIVING

Years ago when I first sat down with a financial planner to help order my life and prepare me for the future, he told me that I needed three savings pockets. He explained that I needed an emergency fund in the bank or with a money market account that was immediately accessible for unexpected emergencies such as car repair or a refrigerator purchase. Then I needed a short-range pocket of savings primarily for college educations for our children. Finally, I needed long-range savings that would be set aside and not touched until I retired. As I matured, I grew every one of those pockets and have found them to be a useful way to manage my money. I am now down to two pockets because all of my children have finished college. I look forward to the day I am down to one, and if you will recommend this book to several thousand of your friends, it will help me greatly.

Most of us have three pockets of giving, as well. The difference is not so much that we create these as I did with my financial planner, but that they just become reality in our lives. Not everyone has saved his or her money the same way, but just about everyone has three pockets available from which he or she can give. The problem is that the church has not learned how to ask for gifts from all three pockets.

THE EARNED-INCOME POCKET

These are monies that we are earning from our salaries or retirement checks. These are the funds that come to us each month that we make decisions about on a regular basis. We buy our groceries, pay our rent and utility bills, and make charitable contributions. These are the monies that sustain our churches and synagogues. It is from this pocket that the preacher encourages persons to tithe or make proportional gifts. By and large the church does a good job of encouraging people to think about this pocket and make a gift from it. The tithing sermon is addressed to this pocket. When the usher passes the plate in front of our noses, the message is to give from this pocket.

We are the envy of the nonprofit world when it comes to the earned-income pocket. Other nonprofit organizations have to have "fund-raisers" to get gifts from this pocket. They will have a car wash, or a bake sale, or a fancy banquet where people are asked to make a contribution to their cause. These are all requests for persons to give them a portion of what they have earned that week.

The church, however, gathers the majority of its donor base every seven days and actually takes a special moment out of that gathering for each donor to give something into the aforementioned plate as an offering.

Now, none of this means that we always do this extremely well or that some solid improvements could not be made in how we seek the first pocket, but we are at least actively seeking gifts from this pocket. Our problem is that we try to meet too many of our needs out of this pocket and leave out the other two.

Quite frequently, I will have a church member say to me, "How can we expect to raise additional money for our new building? We are giving all we can now and we only have a few dollars left over at the end of each year. Where do you think that money will come from?" I try to explain to her that it probably will come from the second and third pockets, which in her church have gone largely untapped.

THE CAPITAL POCKET

This is the pocket that stores our accumulated resources. In it are stocks, bonds, pieces of property, insurance policies, savings accounts, and inheritances we may have received and put away. They are resources that we are certainly going to be held accountable for because they have been entrusted into our care, but they are not a part of our regular cash flow. We do not look into this pocket when we think about going to the movies or buying a new shirt or getting our groceries. Nor is this the pocket we go to when considering what to give to the church each week. These assets were set aside for another purpose. However, those purposes change and the assets are not fully utilized. They wind up just sitting there.

Years ago, my wife and I started a college fund for our children. We put our children through college in the 1990s, when the stock market did extraordinarily well and our fund grew. When all of the children finished, we realized we had some funds still sitting in that account. We had a number of options, such as spending it on ourselves or shifting it over into the retirement side of our savings, or we could give it away. It would have helped our giving if someone had asked us for a gift from that pocket or encouraged us to look there and consider their need.

Also, years ago, I bought some life insurance policies—falling for more than one agent's pitch that whole life was my best guarantee of insurability and protection for my family. I got several policies. Well, those policies have grown substantially over the years, accumulating a cash value. My children no longer need the protection they did when they were young, and our house is nearly paid for. What should I do with these policies that I no longer need?

I could cash them in and donate the cash value. I could change the beneficiary to the church. I could also make a down payment on a lake house. Did anyone in the church offer me any alternatives to think about?

You say, "But we had a capital campaign at our church ten years ago when we were building our sanctuary. Am I supposed to be always building something?"

Of course you are not supposed to be always building a building. But you *are* supposed to be always building the kingdom of God. In the right-hand drawer of every pastor's desk there always should be plans for the future that simply need someone to fund them. From time to time these dreams and plans should be shared with the greater church. Like seed to be scattered, they should be spread out occasionally just to see if they might take root. Doing so will cause individuals to think about their capital pocket and what they might like to do with it on a one-time special occasion.

Some years ago I was involved in a capital campaign with a pastor in a very large church. We had frequently talked about persons in his church who might be available to make significant gifts. Out of the blue one afternoon, he said, "We really should go and see Mr. Jones." I had not heard of this man before and I asked, "Why?" He replied, "Well, about five years ago he came to me and said that he wanted to give one million dollars in memory of his recently departed mother and father. He had inherited the money and he wanted to honor them at the church. I had to tell him that right then we did not have anything on the board where we could use that gift, but if he wanted I could get the trustees together and see what we could come up with. He said he would get back to me."

My jaw just dropped. I knew that we should go and see this man, but I also knew that the chance of him still having one million dollars sitting around to give was pretty slim. Sure enough, when we talked to him about the new building the church was going to build, he said, "Preacher, I sure wish I had known about this earlier. I do not still have the million dollars. I went down to Children's Hospital and talked to them and they told me of a new wing they wanted to build, so I honored Mom and Dad there." We got a check from him. It was for twenty-five thousand dollars.

I frequently ask my seminar crowds, "How many colleges are currently involved in a capital campaign?" They fumble around with one answer or another and then I tell them that *all* of them are currently involved in a campaign. In only a handful are the campaigns public, but every college in the country is in one way or another making its alumni aware of plans and dreams so that if anyone has a capital pocket gift available he or she will know that the college can use it. Colleges do this regularly because they know that if they do not put their foot forward, then someone else will likely reach their donor base first and that gift will be lost forever.

In between the building programs at your church, do you really think your members are sitting on these capital assets just waiting for you to need them? No, they are evaluating every year what to do with them, and if you do not speak up you will not be in their plans.

THE ESTATE POCKET

This is what we will have available to give once we leave this earth. Every one of us will die one day and every church member we are currently serving will also die. Most of us will be richer on that day than we ever were while alive. No longer will we have need of any of the assets in our life, plus we will have added to our barns all that life insurance we have paid premiums on over the years. First the bad news: none of it will be going with us. Now the good news: you aren't going to need it. YOU ARE, HOWEVER, STILL RESPONSIBLE FOR IT. As far as I can figure, God gave you all of those treasures. They were not given to anyone else—just you, and you are responsible as His steward to determine their disposal. The question must be asked of this pocket, just as it should be with the other pockets, "Lord, what do you want me to do with that which you have given me?"

If the answer you come up with to the above-mentioned question is, "Nothing," then try again. Wrong answer! Nowhere in Scripture are we encouraged to do nothing with what God has given us (check out the fate of the servant who buried his master's money). You and I are still accountable; yet a great many Christians choose nothing. Sadly, it seems that the vast majority of our churches support the "nothing" answer because they never talk about this stewardship responsibility with their members.

You might remember that on page 3 I stated that religion receives almost 33 percent of all charitable donations in America. What was not mentioned earlier is that religion only gets 8 percent of all the estate gifts in America, and the ones it gets are much smaller than the gifts to other causes. Whereas religion ranks first as America's favorite charity, it ranks fourth when it comes to bequests. Why would individuals who seemingly love their church more than any other charity fail to remember the church in their will or with a planned gift? The answer is simple. We do not ASK for it. People simply do not think of their church, because the church has been silent on its need or use of these gifts. Less than 10 percent of all the churches in the United States market for planned gifts. The vast majority of clergy never speaks about it or teaches about this responsibility, and in my opinion that is clergy malpractice.

Let me make this as clear as I can. First, everyone has a will. The issue is whether you will write your own or let a court write it for you. If you fail to write one, then you die without a plan, which is just like burying God's treasure in the ground. You take all those assets God has given you such as children, money, property, jewelry, automobiles, dogs, cats, and your favorite pair of cowboy boots and just lay them on the judge's desk and say, " Here, God gave me all this, but you decide what happens now."

God did not give you all that you have for someone to determine its best use. He expects you to decide. To not decide is very irresponsible. It seems that we in the church are supportive of irresponsibility because we are not teaching our people otherwise.

When I teach about estate gifts or planned gifts, as they are often called, I get a lot of the same questions. Some of these are as follows.

"If I ask my people to consider an estate gift or a will gift, doesn't that sound like I want them to die?" Of course not, it is just that you know they WILL die and you have a responsibility to teach them that they are still accountable to the God who gave all that stuff to them. You also have a responsibility to seek ways to grow and build God's church and this is a great way to do it. Now, if you believe that life truly ends at death or that when people die they get to take their toys with them into eternity, then you have other issues that this book isn't prepared to deal with.

"If our church builds up a significant endowment, won't it hurt our annual giving?" Absolutely not, unless you are already receiving the maximum you could ever use for the Kingdom. This problem arises when people set up endowments that have few restrictions and allow the funds to be used for regular, ongoing needs of the church such as salaries or the utility bill. When this happens, pew-sitters get lazy and become welfare religionists (persons who let others pay for their religion). The cure for this is to have in place an endowment policy that restricts us to new ministries, scholarships, maintenance, or capital needs. This lets you do more, and not less, in ministry.

"It just seems that estate gifts and planned giving are very legal and complicated. Can a church really handle these gifts?" The only way you would not be able to handle these gifts is if you cannot handle money, because that is all you have to deal with. Most major denominational groups have foundation professionals who know all the appropriate legal stuff you would get into. All you do is refer your member to this office. The foundation professionals will even write letters for you and provide the correct brochures. All you have to do is decide that this will be taught and get materials mailed. If someone wants to do a charitable remainder trust or a gift annuity or a lead trust, all you have to do is introduce him or her to your denomination's professionals and then wait for the check in the mail. Oh yeah, you do need to say thank you.

In so many ways, planned gifts are the easiest, not the hardest, funds to raise for your church, because someone else will do 90 percent of all the work for you. You must market and you must ask, and then you just sit back and wait for the call that says, "Hello, Reverend, this is Mr.

Jones at your foundation office. Mr. Smith of your church passed away last week and you are the beneficiary of his annuity. Where would you like us to send the check for five hundred thousand dollars?" P. S. Have the address handy!

In a seminar I did last year in Houston at a large downtown church, I posed a question to about 250 clergy and laity in attendance. I asked for all those who had received a letter, a brochure, or some other piece of correspondence from their church asking them to consider a will gift or some other planned gift for the church this year to please raise their hand. Not one hand went up. I then said, "OK, how many of you have received *more* than one letter, brochure, or other piece of correspondence from another nonprofit asking you to consider making a planned gift to them this year?" Two hundred fifty hands went up. Never had I seen such confirmation of why the church is not getting these gifts. We simply aren't asking.

You still think it is difficult? How about this for a marketing strategy? You simply ask each member of your congregation to put one simple sentence in his or her will that says, "After all my bills are paid, I want 10 percent of my estate (a tithe) to go to _____ Church." That is all. You do not have to deal with seminars or regular letters or fancy planned-gift vehicles, just one simple sentence from every member. What could that mean?

Well, the average estate in most of our churches will easily be five hundred thousand dollars (the value of all assets including house, business, insurance, and so on). Let's say that in your church you average twenty funerals a year. If each one of those who died had put that sentence in their will, then your church would receive fifty thousand dollars per person times twenty—one million dollars over the year. You take your million and give it to your denominational foundation and ask them to invest it and send you a check at the end of each year for whatever your million dollars made that year. The average stock market return has been 10 percent, so your church could average one hundred thousand dollars a year FOREVER from *dead* people, and then the next year you would get another one hundred thousand dollars, and the next and the next. Now, you tell me if that would not be better stewardship than "nothing." By the way, if the additional one hundred thousand dollars coming in every year proves to be a burden to you, the foundation will even keep it and put it to use itself.

In one of the last churches that I served, and before I was even close to being as smart as I am now, I was making calls on some members regarding a new sanctuary we were building. After I had visited with one of our older ladies, she asked me if I had been down to visit with Mrs. Brown. I told her no and inquired as to why I should visit Mrs. Brown. Quite indignantly she said, "Because she could build ten of your sanctuaries if she wanted! Her husband left her a sizable sum in a trust account when he died years ago. She is always complaining about how much her taxes are." I was stunned. Mrs. Brown had been a member of our church longer than just about anyone else. She was eighty-two years old, had been a widow for at least ten years, and had never had children. She was still living in the same house she and her husband first moved into sixty-plus years ago. Well, I found time on my schedule to make a visit over there that afternoon. As usual, Mrs. Brown was very cordial and gracious to her preacher. After some chitchat I got right to the point and said, "Mrs. Brown, I understand that your husband left you a sizable amount in a trust fund." She acknowledged it and began to talk about how bad her taxes were. I then asked, "Mrs. Brown, have you ever thought about what will happen to that money once you go to meet Jesus?" To my amazement she said, "Oh yes, I took care of that about two years ago."

My heart sank and I asked, "May I ask what you have decided to do with it?" Again she was most gracious and said, "I am going to give it to the university." I could not understand why. Neither she nor her husband were college graduates and she did not have any children. So I inquired. She simply said, "Well, about two years ago the university president was speaking in town to the Rotary Club and when he finished he came by the house and *asked* me for it." My jaw just dropped. This wonderful lady had been in my church for six decades and neither I nor any other pastor of her church had ever said anything to her about the trust fund. The one who got the gift was the FIRST TO ASK FOR IT. Don't let this happen to you. Ask for the third pocket of giving.

QUESTIONS TO ASK

- What pocket of giving do we feel we are weakest in asking for?
- Do we have an endowment policy and gift acceptance policy in place?
- What might happen if 50 percent of our members actually tithed their wills?

THINGS TO DO

- Invite the director of your denominational foundation to come and assist you in setting up a solid marketing program for planned gifts. If you do not have a denominational foundation, then have the planned-giving officer of a nearby college come in, along with an estate-planning attorney. They can give you all the assistance you need.
- Establish a long-range visioning committee that will always be planning five to ten years in the future and keeping that plan updated for any possible capital donors.

CHAPTER SIX

THE TOP TEN THINGS I WOULD DO NOW

I wish I could give you a list of the top ten things I did right, but I'm afraid I can't do that. Although my churches had excellent stewardship records, I did more things wrong than right. If, however, I could go back, knowing what I know now, there are ten things I would do to raise stewardship in the churches I served. I think they could do the same for your church too.

PRAY, STUDY, AND GET MY ACT TOGETHER FIRST

Most of the churches that I work with are struggling with financial stewardship, and not surprisingly, so is their spiritual leader. I find pastor after pastor who does not have the slightest idea why they believe what they do about stewardship. In fact, many are hard-pressed to even tell me what they believe. There is a great void in stewardship theology and this must be corrected first.

I should not be totally surprised that many of our pastors do not know why they want their churches to be full of giving people, other than the fact that having money in the plate is better than not having money in the plate. I see this same lack of understanding when it comes to why they want persons to worship or why they want people to feed the hungry. It seems like a good idea and the world is a better place if we do these things, but having a solid theology on why is absent.

I am often appalled when I hear television pastors talk about money and how they believe that people must give if they want to be rich, or how they must tithe or they will go to hell. It is abhorrent theology, but at least it is theology. I find that other pastors will often speak against such preaching, but then they offer no alternative nor give a reason that people of faith should do this or that.

The very first thing, then, that I would do if I were a pastor again would be to sit down, pray earnestly for insight, read Scripture on the use of material things along with other books on Christian stewardship, and craft a paper entitled "This Which I Believe about Christian Financial Stewardship." I would put it down and document it as if it were a seminary paper and not a sermon. Then I would move it from a thesis to a sermon and preach it to my congregation. I would hope to help them not just be givers but also be grounded in their giving. From start to finish this might take several months, but like the foundation of a house, once this is done correctly, the rest goes up quickly and solidly.

Once I had firmly grounded myself in my stewardship theology, I would take a hard, practical look at myself. If I believe this, then am I living it? I would explore how I have responded to material possessions in my life and decide what needs to remain and what needs to go. I would specifically explore the role debt is playing in my life and whether it is scriptural or something I need forgiveness for and transformation with. I would get my own giving house in order around the theology I had come to believe is true. I would explore all three pockets of giving and make sure I had made a theologically sound decision about my annual income, my accumulated assets, and my estate.

With all this done, I would then testify. I would stand before the congregation that I had been sent (or called) to lead and share as specifically as I can how I intended to lead them in financial stewardship. I would tell them the amount of my income, including housing, if they did not already know it, and what I intended to give that year. I would tell them of any other assets that I had been blessed with and how I intended to share those for special capital efforts, and I would tell them that I had remembered the church in my will and how I went about it.

You must testify to lead. It is imperative for every pastor. I am aware of the Scriptures admonishing us to go into the closet to pray and not to air our good deeds for all to hear, but I fear these passages are used more to help us escape leadership than to keep us humble. Jesus called us to lead and set an example, and to not do so would be clergy malpractice. We have no right to ask any to do what we are not willing to do ourselves. We do it not to reflect glory on ourselves (sin, sin) but to give glory to God. When our words and actions are done so as to glorify the Master, it is never wrong and, in fact, necessary.

Now, I know that laypersons are reading this book and not just clergy, but you have to understand that the financial stewardship in your church cannot be seriously improved without the active and faithful leadership of your pastor. The laity cannot get it done without the chief shepherd leading them. It is and always will be the pastor who sets the tone about what is important and what the priorities are. It is the pastor who stands before the people every seven days and says, "This is what God wants us to know today." The laity easily picks up on what is crucial and what is not.

Any plan to improve the financial health of your church will then need to begin with the pastor but will not be fully complete without the core of lay leadership standing right beside him or her themselves in witnessing to God's call in their lives to be stewards.

BUILD A HIGH-EXPECTATION CULTURE

When I look at churches that have outstanding financial stewardship, I almost always see a culture that espouses high expectations for its membership in all areas of discipleship and stewardship. I see churches that unabashedly say that all members are expected to attend worship every week that they are well, to serve society in at least one area outside the local church, to be in at least one small group that is studying how to grow as a Christian, and to give at least 10 percent (tithe) of their income. They talk a lot about spiritual disciplines such as prayer and fasting as ways of remaining grounded. Statistics are telling us that these are the churches in America that are growing, and that people tend to leave low-expectation churches to go to high-expectation ones rather than the reverse. If I were starting a church today, I would make it clear that we were going to be high expectation when it came to membership. Those with the idea that following Christ, or marrying Christ to use the biblical analogy of church membership, requires nothing of us would not be a part of my church.

One denomination uses the phrase "Open Hearts, Open Doors, Open Minds" to reflect the kind of church they are. I like it when it is interpreted to mean this is a church that is open to all individuals to come regardless of where they may find themselves. I do not like it when it is interpreted to mean you can walk through the door and not have to have a change of heart or mind as influenced by the grace of God. As the old hymn says, "Just as I am, I come," but as I am, I should not remain.

In much of Christendom today we have so watered down what it means to carry the cross that our members are surprised by any sermon that speaks of expectations and not just cheap grace that requires nothing of us. We cannot buy our salvation or earn it in any way, but to say to people that they can truly enjoy the full fruits of their salvation devoid of accountability is wrong. It cheapens the cross and makes a mockery out of any sense of discipleship.

We must make our expectations clear before persons join the church. This does not mean that they cannot attend every worship service, or come to any class, or receive pastoral care if needed. They can have all those things and we welcome them with open hearts, open doors, and open minds; BUT at the point they want to join the church (marry Christ), they must know ahead of time that there are high expectations.

It is the difference between dating and getting married. While dating you can have a lot of fun and do all sorts of things without serious commitment, because society does not need to have any particular expectations of you to make society work properly. If, however, you get ready to start a family, marriage commitment comes into play and society says that it wants some way to ensure stability for any children brought into it. The two parties and the state agree upon a contract. There are expectations clearly expressed.

Membership in the church can be viewed in much the same way. When someone says they are ready to commit to the body of Christ, a clear set of expectations should be shared and they should not be subtle or ambiguous. Marriage to the church (Christ) should be at least as respected as marriage to a man or a woman. Yet in most cases it is not nearly as demanding as joining the Lion's Club or Rotary.

As I visit in churches across the country, I watch Sunday after Sunday as people come forth and join the church with little or no idea of what they are getting into. I often hear a minister give new members a quick vow such as, "Will you be loyal to the church with prayers, attendance, gifts, and service?" They look at the preacher with a stupid expression and the preacher says, "Oh, your answer is 'I will.'" And they nod. The preacher then wonders why the members are not more committed.

Persons who want to join the church need instruction prior to joining, whether they are joining a church on profession of faith or just transferring. Everyone should have to take a series of classes that explain expectations. These expectations, at a minimum, should be regular attendance, tithing, and service beyond self. These are simple spiritual disciplines that do not save us, but can help keep us in relationship with God.

The biggest argument I get from churches about establishing such classes is that it will cause them to have fewer members. That is correct. It will. You will have fewer people join, but those who do will be prepared to work for the

Kingdom. I have searched the Bible over and nowhere does it say that we are to gauge our effectiveness on the number of members we get into the church. We are, however, called to "make disciples." There is a very high expectancy of making disciples.

Before anyone joined my church, I would have that person come forward with a pledge card and a copy of a service sheet filled in to show where he or she wanted to give himself or herself away. I would take the card and sheet, share with the church that a new disciple had presented himself or herself, tell the church that I had received a financial commitment, and then read where this person was interested in serving. This would reinforce to the old members that this was our priority and that we had high expectations of all. Each member would then reaffirm his or her vows of commitment to the church.

HAVE WEEKLY TESTIMONIES

Nothing helps your members (donors) better understand what their gifts are going toward than testimonies from people who have been touched by your ministry. I would see that at least one testimony is presented to the congregation each week. The best place for this is worship and the backup would be in the newsletter. This testimony need not be longer than two to three minutes, but it needs to be first person and to be as real as possible.

My preferred method would be to have the testimony videotaped the week prior so you could control the time. It is very easy for individuals not used to public speaking to take twenty minutes to say what should have been said in three minutes.

I would have one staff person or a solid lay volunteer take on this task of securing one testimony each week. He or she will certainly get suggestions from other staff or church members, but one person needs to be accountable for it. This person can also help the testifier know what is expected and how to go about sharing in the time allotted.

I believe the best time to have the testimony is immediately prior to when the offering is going to be collected. Some of our churches will take two to three minutes to ask, "Will the ushers please come forward as we receive our morning tithe and offering?" (Ever notice that it is usually framed as a question, as if someday the ushers might say, "No, we will not come forward.") As the ushers slowly make their way to get the plates, line up, and walk, the pastor stands alone at the front smiling quietly at people. It really gives the impression in many services that someone has just shouted, "Time-out" for worship. Once the ushers get to the front, a prayer is offered and then some organist plays funereal music. It is, indeed, much like an intermission at a drama.

Instead of this slow, monotonous ritual that tells no one why you deserve the support you are currently seeking, substitute one person sharing a testimony on how she or he has witnessed the church at work. It could be an elderly lady sharing how she was cared for after the recent death of her husband. It could be a Sunday-school teacher sharing a remark from a young student that showed that the student "got it." It could be a youth talking about the impact a mission trip had on his life. It needs to be a story that testifies to the power of the spirit in the world today and how the church has been the vehicle from which that spirit has operated.

The testimony should never quote numbers or statistics. Saying, "We have had a 5 percent increase in the number of youth on Sunday night" does not tell me anything. Professional wrestling has been getting great crowds too. What is happening to the lives of these young people is what I want to know about.

As I said, I believe that the best forum for this is in worship, where a person's face and sincerity can be seen. However, I would not stop there. I would ask the person to elaborate on his or her story, and then I would print it in the newsletter and put it on your website. Bottom line—you cannot tell your stories too much. Quit keeping what you have a secret and get it out there.

At one of the churches that I was doing a stewardship audit for I recommended that they hire one part-time staff person who would do nothing other than secure testimonies from church members, put these on video, and get a written story. They initially rebelled because of the cost and wondered about its value. After some wrangling, they moved forward in an ambitious way. Today they have a website dedicated to these stories and never publish anything without a story in it. Their financial reports are now testimonies of faith. After doing this for one year they had a surplus in their multimillion-dollar budget for the first time in more than a decade, and they report that numerous new people have chosen the church to be their home simply because of the testimonies they have read on the website.

Remember, the number one reason people choose to make a gift is a belief in the mission. These testimonies will tell them better than any other way that you are fulfilling yours.

HAVE REGULAR, ONGOING CHRISTIAN FINANCIAL PLANNING CLASSES

I can still see the face of the young man after worship one Sunday. He was waiting in the back of the sanctuary until I had finished shaking several hundred hands. The sermon had been on tithing, and as was my custom, I had not held much back in my impassioned plea for my people to respond to God's call to give. I listened to a grumble or two from some of my folk, but by this time most knew how important I thought tithing was and they had received the sermon well. This young man, however, had a reaction I had not seen before when I had preached on Christian financial stewardship. He was weeping. It was not a big BOO HOO, but his eyes were wet and his lower lip was quivering. He was wiping his eyes as needed with his handkerchief. I assumed that he had experienced some great personal loss and just being in worship had been painful for him in some way.

I went over to him ready to console him in his loss but I was not prepared for what I heard when I got to him. "Preacher, your sermon really got to me today," he said. I looked quizzically at him and inquired, "On tithing?" Then he sat down and began to speak: "Pastor, I listened to everything you had to say and it was not the first time I had heard that God's command for my life is to at least tithe. Even my daddy told me that I was to save 10 percent, give God 10 percent, and I could have discretion with the rest. I know what is right and what is wrong. Today you challenged those of us who were not tithing to start this week. I want to. I really want to, but I do not know how." He paused a moment and then went on: "You know that I just started out at the plant and it is going to take me a while to work my way up. My wife is teaching school. We have our two girls in day care and you know that Susie has asthma, which has cost us a lot in medical bills. Well, Pastor, I have not managed things very well. We got this new house when our second child was born and then a van to carry everyone around. I let things get out of hand and used credit cards for too many things and now we owe nearly forty thousand dollars to six different credit card companies. It is ruining our life and I do not know how to get out of this mess. I am not tithing. In fact, I have not given the church anything all year. Pastor, I know I am not doing the right thing, but I do not know what to do with this mess." The tears really flowed then.

I felt awful. I had just spent twenty minutes of pounding from God's pulpit on this young man and I had offered him no answers—just condemnation. He deserved better than his pastor had given him. I told him that I wanted him to give me a couple of days and I would be calling him with some answers regarding how to get his stewardship life in order. We prayed together and parted company.

The next morning I started doing some homework. I realized that what I had just done was in essence like condemning people for not reading the Bible but never telling them how to get a Bible, or condemning them for not serving in missions without giving them mission opportunities. I told this young man to tithe without offering him any tools to help him do exactly that. I would try to do better.

I found several wonderful teaching tools that do not just explain scriptural giving but also help persons organize all their material life around Christian principles. I found out that all of them have wonderful, easy-to-understand workbooks and teaching videos, alleviating the need for Christian financial planning professionals to be in every church. They were all reasonably priced and just needed me to determine which ones would best suit my congregation's needs.

These programs are:

- Crown Financial Ministries (http://www.crown. org/)
- Master Your Money (http://www.masteryour money.org/)
- Financial Peace University (http://www.daveram sey.com/fpu/home/)
- Good Sense (http://www.goodsenseministry.com/)
- Abundant Living (http://www.abundantliving ministry.org/ministrypartners.aspx)

All of the above are excellent, and every one of them will help your people learn how to be generous Christian givers in the real world.

We pastors must accept the reality that a huge number of our members are in serious financial jeopardy. It is estimated today that the average credit card debt in America is nine thousand dollars. When the interest rates are sometimes above 20 percent, a large credit card debt can be devastating. Remember, we are to accept people as they are (in debt and in sin) and then help them be what God wants them to be. These classes can be a big help.

What I would do is choose one that I thought best fit my church and get the core leadership of my church to go through the program. Then I would get them to make this class part of our new-member training, so that it would just become a part of our new-member expectations.

If you just decide to offer the class and put up a flyer, you will not have a great response. People are reluctant to expose themselves by attending such a class. It is like classes on marriage. When the church just sets one up and says come if you like, not as many will take part as if you set it up for new members and any others who are interested. Even though many members of the congregation may be struggling with their marriages, they do not want everyone to know it. When you have the class as a part of who you are as a church family and mandate that all new people go, you will find that your established members will soon gravitate to the class.

I would plan on offering, at a minimum, one class every quarter, and when one ended I would be sure to get a testifier up before offering the next one.

I have also found two other books that may be extremely helpful in growing a culture of giving in a congregation. The first is *The Treasure Principle* by Randy Alcorn. The other is *Fields of God* by Andy Stanley. I like them because they are small, one hundred-page books and very simple to read. Either one would make an excellent text for getting the entire congregation dialoguing about how giving relates to their lives. One pastor I know purchased a copy of *Fields of God* for each family in his church and mailed it to each one using his own funds. Each copy cost him $3.50, but he reported that nothing has ever made such a difference in the congregation's giving. Don't get hung up on every little thing that is said in these books. Neither author claims divine authority, but they sure do a good job of simplifying the biggest problem we have with our congregations.

PREACH DIRECTLY ON MONEY FOUR TIMES A YEAR

At a capital campaign meeting last year we were nearing the end of a session with the steering committee when one of the members asked me when I was going to preach on money. I asked him what he meant and he said, "You know, when are you going to get up in the pulpit and tell our people they need to give?" I replied to him that I did not plan on preaching, at least in the campaign, and had every confidence his pastor could handle that part of our campaign. His reply was all too familiar, "We really don't like for our pastor to talk about money from the pulpit. It will be much better if you do it." Sadly, the minister spoke up quickly and said, "Don't worry; I don't plan on doing any preaching about money." This pastor is a very good man, and a very effective preacher from what his members tell me, but money is a topic that he avoids. His campaign underperformed.

We know why his members did not want him to address the topic of using money, and we know why the pastor did not want to speak about it. I am not at all sure that either reason is biblically sound.

Members grumble when they hear sermons dealing with their greatest sin. They did it to Jesus, to Paul, to the prophets, and to the disciples. People would much rather sit and hear a story of how loved they are and how precious they are in God's sight than to hear that they have fallen short of the glory of God. It began with Adam. When he was first created, he loved being in communion with God, but once sin crept in he went and hid. We don't want God to see our shortcomings and we do not want our preacher on Sunday morning reminding God of what those shortcomings are.

As a pastor I sure did like getting compliments more than getting complaints. I ate it up on Sundays when my members would come out and pat me on the back and tell me what a wonderful job I had done. It did not feel quite the same when they came out and had their heads slightly bowed so as not to make eye contact. Subconsciously, I wanted to preach so that the crowd would pat me on the back. I knew when a sermon was going to cause some furor—and one on the use of money would usually do it— and my stomach was always a bit tighter that morning.

Many of my clergy friends have heard the joke of the young seminarian beginning his ministry at his first church. After the initial sermon, where he preached against tobacco use, one of his lay leaders took him aside to remind him that he was preaching in Kentucky and tobacco was loved by many a farmer in that church. The next Sunday the seminarian chose to preach against hard liquor. Again the layman took him aside and reminded him that he was in Kentucky and many of his members worked at a local distillery. His third sermon dealt with gambling and especially horseracing. Once again the layman came to the seminarian and said that he could not preach on that either. After all, had he not heard of the Kentucky Derby? Finally, exasperated, he asked the helpful layman what he could talk about. The reply: "Next Sunday preach on the evils of voodoo in Haiti. Everyone will like that."

In churches where I consistently see exemplary stewardship, its importance is evidenced in the preaching done in that church. The members will tell you that they are reminded on a regular basis of the centrality of stewardship to the Christian faith. People who come to visit hear that it is important, and when those people decide which church to join, they know how important stewardship is to the one they chose.

I believe that planning to preach on the use of money on four occasions each year is about right. That is 7 percent of all your Sundays. As almost all of you know, it is much less than the percentage of time Jesus talked about it. I would be sure to preach on financial stewardship on one of the first Sundays in January, which is the time when people are rethinking priorities for the year, once during Lent, once in the summer, and then once in mid-November as persons are thinking about Thanksgiving. Yes, you will probably have some members say to you that all they hear are sermons on money, but you will know that you preached forty-five other messages. I wonder why they do not remember them the same way.

When I say, "preach," I mean that the theme of the message deals with materialism and the use of money. Just slipping in the words *tithing* or *giving* in some other sermon will not have nearly the same effect. Your people will know what you feel is a priority and what is not nearly as important. Also, guard against using humor in such a way that subtly says to your congregation that you do not mean this. Your people are looking for clues as to what is important in the Christian life and what is not. When you talk about financial stewardship, let them know you mean every word of it.

TARGET MARKET YOUR CORRESPONDENCE

I would get my staff to divide my congregation into separate groupings so I could target each one most effectively, for example, with mail messages or special meetings. I would create the following groups for marketing purposes: tithers; growing Christians (those giving regularly but not tithing yet); contributors (those who give something at least once a year); nongivers. I would also have my staff make a division of generations, separating builders, Boomers, and Gen Xers.

How do you know who the tithers are? I would let my congregation self-identify. Over a period of weeks I would provide a card for them to fill out, which among other things would let them check that they were currently tithing. You will find that 90 percent of your tithers will let you know and sign their name to the card. Your treasurer or financial secretary can usually determine the others. Each year you update your list of tithers and publish it in your newsletter with something like: *Tithing Counts. This year we have increased the number of tithers in our church from forty-four to sixty-one. If you have moved up to tithing this year, please let us know so we can add you to the pastor's list.*

Having this division will let you communicate very effectively with your people. With the tithers you can send a special thank-you note two or three times a year. You can host a dinner at your home and invite them just to say thanks. As for the other groups, you can work directly with them to encourage a move up to the next level. The growing Christians can get correspondence encouraging them to make the move to tithing. The once-a-year giver could get special material on how to use electronic fund transfer to make a regular gift instead of a periodic one. Those who are not giving can get material that encourages them to just start making a gift, perhaps to a special project.

It is important to remember that one of the real benefits of having the congregation divided like this is planning pastoral care. If a person is not giving, this is a clear signal that their soul is sick. It is our responsibility to care for that soul and keep it from dying. The pastoral team or shepherd team of the church should regularly review those families who have not given and determine how best to minister to them. At this point it is not at all about money. It is about saving souls.

Many churches have boards up on the wall with a list of those who are currently in the hospital or sick. I believe that a similar board should also be up in the office area with the names of those persons who are not giving so that the staff can be reminded to pray for them and not let them slip away from Christ.

SPEND MORE TIME WITH MAJOR DONORS

It surprises me that pastors seem so reluctant to spend special time with people who have significant wealth and have chosen to give it to the church. They are in great fear that someone will accuse them of "treating some members differently." We have previously gone over this, but of course each pastor should treat members differently because they are different. Our job is and has always been to take people where they are and lead them closer to Christ.

It is also our job to help people use their gifts and graces for the good of the church, the body of Christ. Spending time with persons of wealth who have already expressed in their giving a desire to serve is a way to do our job.

I believe each pastor should intentionally invite the top five to ten donors to his or her home about three times a year. The purpose of this visit is twofold. One, it is so you can directly say thank you to those who make ministry happen with their giving, and two, it is to listen as they share their hopes and dreams for the future.

I have seen some great things come from these meetings. People always appreciate being thanked and it is nice to know that the head of your church recognized the importance of your gift and directly thanked you. When something feels good, people naturally work to continue whatever it was that brought that good feeling.

The other neat thing that often occurs is that these people get to talking about what they would like to see the church doing, and before the night is out you have your top-ten donors all on the same page wanting to make something happen. That can be a very powerful force for positive change. They also take heart in seeing that others who have obviously invested a lot are on their side. When you have your top-ten donors all lined up in support of an idea, that idea is not likely to be stopped.

In far too many meetings, it is the person who is not invested who spends most of the time mouthing off and gathering up a head of steam for usually stopping ministry from progressing. It can easily give the false impression that something does not have much support. In this gathering everyone knows that the other is invested and she or he can feel the support from the "doers" in the room. One word of caution: do not use this time as a way to sell your agenda. This is a time for you to say thanks and to listen. If you bring them together and it appears that they have just become a captive audience for one of your ideas, it can easily go sour on you. Don't be surprised, however, if their agenda falls pretty close to yours once it is all said and done. It will just have originated with them and that makes it better.

People who are not invited to this gathering will criticize you as being a pastor who caters to the rich folk. Not true. You spend special time with a lot of different groups, such as those who sing in the choir, those who have suffered a loss, and those who work with the youth or teach Sunday school. What makes those who give any less worthy a group? Remember, any pastor who treats all of his or her members the same is committing clergy malpractice, because members *are* different.

WRITE TEN THANK-YOU NOTES A WEEK

I still remember some of the thank-you notes that I received as a pastor. I was really touched by the one that two newlyweds sent me about a week after I performed their wedding. I had not done anything extraordinary, in my opinion. We had met for several sessions of premarital counseling, had a nice rehearsal, and then a beautiful spring wedding with reception. The note had obviously taken them some thought as they mentioned specifically what had been done that they felt was so helpful. I had not done the wedding so I would get such a note, but it surely felt good to realize that they had noticed the time and energy I had put in.

I got a note from a member of a congregation I had helped raise considerable funds to build their new education complex. She really appreciated the attitude that was reflected in our meetings and especially some of the prayers that were offered. She noted the spiritual struggle she had entered into and how gratified she felt with her gift. She said she just had to write and express her thanks. I had not worked with her church so that persons would write me notes, and I probably would have worked just as hard without a note, but it surely did feel good to be so recognized by this fine woman.

All of us have memories of getting heartfelt thank-you notes, yet we write so few of them to our members. We watch silently each Sunday as hundreds drop money in a plate. We witness countless numbers teaching classes or sitting in a nursery so Momma and Daddy can go to a class. We wave good-bye from the parking lot as groups head off on mission trips or to build a Habitat for Humanity house. But we seldom write personal notes and express our thanks.

In my seminars I like to ask how many of the laity present have gotten a thank-you note from their pastor in the last five years. The answer is usually zero. These are most often some of the finest church members that pastor has and yet they have not been thanked in at least five years. I ask them if they have ever gotten a personal note thanking them for any monetary gift they have made. Again, the answer is usually zero. Then I ask them if they have volunteered for another nonprofit or made a gift to a nonprofit and if so how many have gotten personal thank-you notes. Dozens of hands go up. Our competition is thanking the same people we are ignoring. This must change.

I would set aside fifteen minutes at the same time each week to write ten thank-you notes. These are to be personal and handwritten on a note card. They don't need to be more than five or six sentences long and should all fit on one side of the card. They can be sent to people who have been teaching, serving, or giving. The rule is that no fewer than ten get written at the same time every week. Over the course of a year you will have written 520 thank-you notes to your members. The impact will be amazing.

As a part of the ten, you can count any thank-you note you send to someone who has just made an extraordinary gift to the church. Advise the treasurer that you want to be notified no later than Monday morning of any gift that was out of the ordinary so you can personally thank the giver in a letter and later in person, if you get the chance. The stories of people who gave again simply because the charity they gave to truly appreciated the gift the first time are too numerous to mention, but entire colleges have been formed simply from a thank-you.

An e-mail will not substitute. I know that it is the most convenient and comfortable way to communicate these days, but when it comes to truly expressing thanks, you cannot beat a handwritten letter or note that showed you took time to really care.

Write ten a week and then see how many times a week you wind up getting thanked for expressing sincere thanks.

REVIEW INDIVIDUAL GIVING ONCE A MONTH

A few years ago I was reviewing the giving records at a church I would soon be working with and I came across the name of a person I had not encountered before. He was giving more than one hundred thousand dollars a year to the operating budget, which ranked him second in giving at this church. I asked the pastor about this family. He did not know to whom I was referring. He wanted to do some research and call me back. When he did, he told me this was a family who had joined the church about six months previously and he had not had the chance to get to know them. He gave me the name of another staff member who knew them better. Working with that staff member we were able to meet with the family and received the second highest gift in the campaign. But we almost missed them!

If the church had not been involved in a capital campaign where the consultant would be reviewing the giving records, I do not know how long it might have been before the pastor or other staff was made aware of what potentials were there. It would not have been unusual if this donor felt unappreciated and left for a church that acted as though they really needed him.

Those checks that this family was dropping in the plate were loud signals about what was important to them. We cannot afford to let months or years go by without being aware of families like this. Pastors have an obligation to help people contribute in the best way possible for the good of the Kingdom.

Can you imagine the uproar if the lead singer of the Metropolitan Opera had been sitting in the congregation for six months just singing hymns and no one from the church staff approached her to sing in worship? In fact, you probably would have had a dozen members come up to the pastor after just one service and comment about the incredible voice they had heard in the pews. They would be encouraging someone to go find that person and use her to make worship as strong as possible. What's the difference in finding someone who needs to share the gift of song and finding someone who needs to share the gift of wealth?

The difference is that when people come to the pastor and encourage him or her to call on the great singer, they know they will not be called on because they do not have the gift of song. However, if they encourage the pastor to call on people with money, it could mean that he or she will be calling on them and their sin will be exposed. Therefore, when they hear that the pastor is visiting with persons of wealth or singling them out in any way, they protest, not out of a sense of holy priorities, but out of a sense of shame. Do not let this attitude run your church!

As mentioned earlier, we have very few insights into the hearts of people. It is so easy to assume that the real saints are in one particular group when that is not even close to the truth. They talk a good game and they are always around, but when it comes to genuinely carrying the cross and walking the walk, they are nowhere to be found. You did not truly know the character of the disciples until Calvary when only one chose to be present. The others just could not risk it.

Giving is the closest thing we have on a daily basis to getting a true picture of a person's character. It is in giving that individuals must make a conscious decision to risk that which they value greatly. When you see them overcome the fear of parting with that which the world values so much, then you know Jesus must have their heart.

This is what you learn when you regularly review giving records for insights to help you do your work as a pastor. You can see if a certain class that people are taking is having an impact because you can see what has happened to their decision to give. You may not be able to see how they are living their lives at work or home. You will not notice if they party a bit differently, but you can see concretely if their giving has changed and learn how to create that change in others.

What if you see someone is suddenly giving less? You do the same thing that a businessperson would do when a good customer all of a sudden stops placing orders anymore. You would contact him or her and find out what is going on. Remember, unlike the businessperson, your main concern is not the money but the soul. The rapid falling off of a giving pattern can tell you of a crisis in someone's life that you might not have known about. It can highlight how pastoral care needs to best be extended. If you were not reviewing these records regularly, then a crisis may have escalated to the point where the church could not effectively intervene and help.

I simply cannot find any reason for a pastor to not establish as a regular practice reviewing the giving records once a month. The only reason I have ever heard as to why it should not be done goes back to a pastor who knew and in some way abused the privilege and told others about something that should have been confidential. That is wrong and should be dealt with appropriately by the superiors of that pastor. If a pastor tells others about giving records or counseling sessions or anything confidential, then that pastor should be disciplined. However, all the future pastors should not be forbidden to do counseling or to know the giving records. This would be as stupid as a bank forbidding all their employees from handling money because one had stolen from them in the past.

NEVER SEND OUT A LINE-ITEM BUDGET AGAIN

For more than twenty years as a pastor I would help prepare and mail out the obligatory line-item budget. I did not want my members to think we were hiding anything. On it I would show every category we would be recording our expenses in, from utilities, to insurance, to every single salary (usually broken down to expenses, housing, retirement, and so on).

I understood the budget and was generally proud of it. It took me years to realize that it was a real turnoff for my donor members. They would take the budget and on a quick glance see that salaries were taking up more than 50 percent of the budget. Then they would see that with our building debt, maintenance, and insurance we were spending another 15 percent just on facilities. They would then see that another 15 percent was going to the denomination to pay for headquarters personnel and retirement benefits, among other things.

That would leave about 20 percent that appeared to be ministry. It was no wonder that each year after sending it out I would hear one gripe after another about the budget. I thought it was from people who did not want to give, but now realize that many of those complaining were individuals who wanted to give and were deciding not to give to the church because they were not sure the money would be used wisely.

Once I started working with nonprofits, I noticed that none of them ever sent line-item budgets out. They would produce one for the board to use and for internal accounting purposes, but they never—and I mean never—mailed it to all their donors. I asked why and got a simple answer, "It is not helpful and it is not necessary. Our donors cannot tell who we are and what we do by a line-item budget. We produce a lot of material detailing what we are doing in accomplishing our mission and what it costs, but not by using a line-item budget. It doesn't tell anyone how we are changing lives."

I looked at some of my old budgets and realized the nonprofits were absolutely right. When I looked at worship, for instance, it appeared that we did very little in worship. We had a line item for it, but it was only a few thousand dollars to cover bulletins and replace paraments. Yet we had more than one hundred fifty worship services that year. To be accurate and help my congregation understand the worship budget, I needed to share what worship really costs, and that would take in a percentage of my salary, my secretary's salary, and the music director's salary, plus a percentage of utilities and maintenance and insurance. All these things are necessary for us to have worship for the thousands who attend, yet my line-item budget seemed to say it was a low priority for us.

We need to cease sending out line-item budgets and prepare what I call a missional budget. This budget takes the church's mission of worship, nurture, service, and evangelism and then divides the entire budget into those categories. Why? Because the number one reason people give is a belief in your mission. You must explain how you are accomplishing that mission to get support. The other reason is that 99 percent of your members really don't care about the line items. They just want to know if you are changing lives with the money given to you.

This is not hard to do. You will have to do a bit of research to divide up salaries into mission areas, but it can be done. For instance, what percent of the pastor's time goes for worship, evangelism, nurture, and so forth? Then add that part of his or her salary to that area.

You can and should produce a line-item budget and make people aware that it is in the office for anyone who wants to see it so no one will think you are hiding things. What you will find is that about two people a year will actually want to see it, and generally they are up to no good.

To explain what I mean, see the difference in the two budgets noted below. They are from the same church, but they are sharing their ministry in two very different ways.

LINE-ITEM BUDGET

First Church Annual Budget
"Changing Lives for Christ"

Income

Pledges	$150,000
Nonpledged contributions	$30,000
Sunday-school offering	$5,000
Christmas Eve	$5,000
Interest	$10,000
Total	**$200,000**

Expenses

Operations:

Utilities	$8,000
Maintenance	$5,000
Postage	$5,000
Office Supplies	$3,000
Insurance	$8,000
Copier	$2,000
Telephone	$2,500
Janitorial Supplies	$2,000
Subtotal	*$35,500*

Programs:

Music	$1,500
Stewardship	$100

Missions	$500
Children's Ministry	$1,000
Youth Ministry	$1,000
Adult Ministry	$500
Boy Scouts	$500
Archives	$400
Subtotal	*$5,500*

Conference/Cooperative Giving:

Support Services	$12,000
World Missions	$10,000
Russian Initiative	$5,000
Retired Pastor Fund	$5,000
Subtotal	*$32,000*

Staff:

Pastor	$50,000
Pastor Utilities	$4,000
Pastor Expense	$10,000
Pastor Insurance	$10,000
Secretary	$20,000
Music Director (PT)	$10,000
Youth Director (PT)	$6,000
Pulpit Supply	$2,000
Continuing Education	$5,000
Janitor	$10,000
Subtotal	*$127,000*

Total Budget	**$200,000**

MISSIONAL BUDGET

First Church Annual Budget
"Changing Lives for Christ"

Your church leadership has constructed a bold plan of ministry to continue our mission of changing lives for Christ. We celebrate a wonderful past year but commit ourselves to even more lives coming to Christ in the new one. Join us in this journey of being God's people in Cityville.

Our Plan of Ministry

A. To provide meaningful, life-changing worship every week of the year.

Last year we held 112 worship services where, on an average week, 190 people gathered to praise God and hear His Word. Fourteen persons gave their life to Christ for the first time in those services and nine rededicated themselves to serving the Master. The Special Music events of Easter and Christmas Eve had more than one hundred persons in attendance who were unchurched. One young man joined the church after one of these special services and was baptized. He said it was only the second time he'd been in a church in his life. Today he's volunteering time with our high-school students.

Next year we plan to add a junior choir with at least twelve third through sixth graders. Already we're planning for them to sing on Palm Sunday. A new praise team is being trained, and a second service is tentatively planned to begin in September. We want to increase our attendance to 220 and double the number of first-time commitments of faith.

Budget Total—$80,000

(This total includes a percentage of the pastor's salary; the pastor's utilities, expenses, and insurance; the secretary, music director, and janitor's salaries; staff continuing education; janitor; the children's and music ministries; janitorial supplies; telephone; copier; insurance maintenance; and utilities.)

B. To nurture persons in their faith journey.

Our church has never been one to feel that once a dedication to Christ was made we were finished *or* that God was finished. It is the reason that we spend a lot of energy and prayer seeking to determine how to help all persons grow in their relationship with the Lord, whether they are three years old or ninety-three years old.

Last year we served an average of seventy-two persons in our Sunday-school classes. Additionally, we had twelve people complete DISCIPLE Bible Study I, and eight new members completed the Alpha course. Our vacation Bible school, with forty-nine children present, was the largest in our history. Our youth group, which was nearly nonexistent at the start of the year, grew to averaging thirteen youth each Sunday night for United Methodist Youth Fellowship (UMYF). For the first time ever, we offered Abundant Living as a Christian financial planning tool for our families, and fifteen of them completed the program.

Our hopes for the new year are to add one additional children's class and begin an adult small group program that would meet during the week. We want to continue the success of DISCIPLE, Alpha, and Abundant Living by offering at least one class of each. It is expected that we can enlarge our UMYF by at least another five young persons and add a mission trip to their educational experience next summer.

Budget Total—$37,000

(This total includes a percentage of the pastor's salary; the pastor's utilities, expenses, and insurance; the secretary and janitor's salaries; the youth director's salary; children, adult, and youth ministry; telephone; copier; utilities; maintenance; Boy Scouts; and so on.)

C. To witness to our faith in service beyond ourselves.

First Church has always been conscious of the fact that Jesus said, "Go into all the world." We see ourselves as servants and laborers in a vineyard that does not belong to us. In this past year we joined with many of our sister and brother churches in supporting missions worldwide through our cooperative program. We had a hand in sending out three hundred missionaries to every continent except Antarctica. We helped feed the hungry, clothe the naked, and bring safe water to those who had never had it. Last year also saw us involved in the Russian Initiative for the first time. Two of our members joined a mission team in going to Russia to help plant a new church. This new church now has sixty-eight members, all persons who had no church involvement before. Forty-one families used our clothes-and-food closet during the year.

Next year we hope to enlarge the numbers of those helping plant the church in Russia and to add a work team to the denominational task force building houses in Louisiana. We will certainly continue to fully support our cooperative program and ministries 100 percent.

Budget Total—$83,000

(This total includes a percentage of the pastor's salary; pastor's utilities, expenses, and insurance; the secretary and janitor's salaries; telephone; copier; utilities; maintenance; support services; World Missions; Russian Initiative; Retired Pastor Fund; missions; and so on.)

Total needed to fulfill our mission of "Changing Lives for Christ": $200,000

A detailed line-item budget is available in the church office for any who wish to review it.

A SPECIAL WORD TO PASTORS

As I read over much of what I have written in this book, I am a bit overcome by how much of it is pointed directly at the pastor. As I read chapter after chapter I began to feel a bit guilty for adding more weight onto shoulders that are already called upon to carry so much. I shared the life of church pastor with many of you for a number of years, and when I ceased to practice my ministry in that way it was truly at a time when I did not think I had one thing left to give. Each year following my years of seminary it seemed that ministry got harder and harder and the expectations grew exponentially. God must have seen my fatigue and opened up the door of Horizons to give me a chance to remain in ministry but in a very different capacity. Thanks be to God!

When I finished my seminary education, I came out basically with the instructions that if I would preach the gospel well on Sunday mornings and care for my people who were sick and shut in during the week, I would have a happy and fruitful ministry. I found out differently almost immediately. Right off, my first church expected me to be a builder and lead them to relocate. I was now going to be judged on how well I could get this job done. In my succeeding church they also needed building, but they needed a total revamping of their youth department as well and, without the resources to hire a professional, they looked to me to be that expert. No one said I could preach less or visit less, either. In my next place of service, they not only wanted all that I had done before, but added the need to be led in mission involvement, and looked to me to carry them on foreign mission excursions. The pressures to be good at more and more things just seemed to grow all the time, and about the time I thought I was getting the hang of one thing, a new expectation would arise.

Many of you are reading this book and now feeling, *Oh gosh, he expects us to now be fund-raising experts as well.* The weight on your back just multiplied manyfold. I would not blame you if you just threw the book away and said, "Enough already! I can't take one more responsibility on top of what I already have. If I had wanted to deal with money, I would have chosen another occupation. I want to change lives for Christ, not count money." I understand fully.

I do not know one pastor, including myself, who said, "I really like raising money, so I am going to go into the pastoral ministry." I think if I did ever hear that, I would question not only that person's commitment to ministry, but also his or her sanity. It may help you to see that Christian financial stewardship is not another one of the things we have to do. It truly is to be who we are.

A lot of us are not good builders, or good youth workers, or good children's ministry people. We are not all good preachers or visitors. Some of us have a good bedside manner and some of us have a lousy one. Many of us can organize a great meeting and others of us cannot organize our own desk. Some of us are great leaders with staff but a lot of us would prefer to be left completely alone with no one to supervise. God has wonderfully and thoughtfully made us all with a different set of gifts and graces. Praise God!

However, we are all called to be stewards. Every one of us as his creation has been given by the Creator dominion over His earth and all that is in it. We are all equally called to be appropriate stewards. It is not something we do. It is who we are.

My words to those of you who have been given a church to serve is for you to add not one more JOB to your day planner, but simply make stewardship the hallmark of who you are each and every day. This means you manage your time as God would have you manage it. It means that you guide the children He has blessed you with in ways that are pleasing to Him. It means that you do not spoil the air and soil that He has allowed you to live with. And it means that you spend, save, and give the money that came from Him in a way that He would want it done—and then share how you are doing it with the congregation given to you. It really should not be one more thing you do, but simply who you are as a child of God.

I am absolutely convinced that pastoral ministry in the twenty-first century is the hardest job on earth. To do it well and to do it right is nearly impossible. This text is certainly not meant to make that job any more of a burden than it already is, but to hopefully enable clergy and laity alike to see how they can better be what the Creator has made them to be.

SUGGESTIONS FOR FURTHER READING

Below are some selected books that I feel will help any church or pastor grow in an understanding of financial stewardship. It is a long way from an exhaustive list, but it is one that I feel is thorough enough to help anyone move beyond where they are now.

CHRISTIANS AND MONEY

Alcorn, Randy. *The Treasure Principle*. New York: Random House, 2001.

Barna, George. *How to Increase Giving in Your Church*. Ventura, Calif.: Regal Press, 1997.

Christopher, Clif, and Herb Mather. *Holy Smoke*. Nashville: Disciple Resources, 1999.

Durall, Michael. *Beyond the Collection Plate*. Nashville: Abingdon Press, 2003.

Hoge, Dean, Patrick McNamara, and Charles Zech. *Plain Talk about Churches and Money*. Bethesda: Alban Institute, 1997.

Jeavons, Thomas, and Rebekah Basinger. *Growing Givers' Hearts*. San Francisco: Jossey-Bass, 2000.

Joiner, Donald. *Creating a Climate for Giving*. Nashville: Disciple Resources, 2001.

Mather, Herb. *Don't Shoot the Horse*. Nashville: Discipleship Resources, 1994.

Mead, Loren. *Financial Meltdown in the Mainline*. Bethesda: Alban Institute, 1998.

Miller, Herb. *Full Disclosure*. Nashville: Discipleship Resources, 2006.

Reeves, Michael. *Extraordinary Money*. Nashville: Discipleship Resources, 2002.

Reeves, Michael, Rob Fairly, and Sanford Coon. *Creative Giving*. Nashville: Discipleship Resources, 2005.

Reeves, Michael, and Jennifer Tyler. *Faith and Money*. Nashville: Discipleship Resources, 2004.

Schaller, Lyle. *The New Context for Ministry*. Nashville: Abingdon Press, 2002.

Slaughter, Michael. *Money Matters*. Nashville: Abingdon Press, 2006.

Stanley, Andy. *Fields of Gold*. Carol Stream, Ill.: Tyndale, 2004.

FUND-RAISING

If you want to improve your skills as a fund-raiser, below is a starting list of books I would recommend.

Drucker, Peter F. *Managing the Nonprofit Organization*. New York: HarperCollins, 1990.

Heetland, David. *Fundamentals of Fund Raising*. Nashville: Abingdon Press, 1989.

Panas, Jerold. *Born to Raise*. Chicago: Bonus Books, 1988.

———. *Mega Gifts*. Chicago: Bonus Books, 1984.

Rosso, Henry. *Rosso on Fund Raising*. San Francisco: Jossey-Bass, 1996.

Sturtevant, William. *The Artful Journey*. Chicago: Bonus Books, 1997.